DATE DUE

JUL 19 '7	JUN 18 '75		
JUL 26 '7	OCT 29 '7		
NOV 7 '7	DEC 12 '7		
FEB 28 '73	MAR 25 '7		
MAY 2 '7	OCT 19 '77		
MAY 9 '73	JUN 4 '80		
JUN 8 '73			
NOV 7 '7	OCT 22 '7		
FEB 20	NOV 2		
NOV 27 '74	JUN 5		
DEC 04 '74	JUN 19 '8		
	MAR 23 '88		

Experimental Dance

Other books in this series:

Experimental Painting
by Stephen Bann

Experimental Architecture
by Peter Cook

Experimental Theatre
From Stanislavsky to Today
by James Roose-Evans

Experimental Cinema
by David Curtis

Experimental Dance

John Percival

UNIVERSE BOOKS
New York

Published in the United States of America in 1971
by Universe Books
381 Park Avenue South, New York, N.Y. 10016
and in Great Britain in 1971 by
Studio Vista Limited, Blue Star House,
Highgate Hill, London, N19

Library of Congress Catalog Card Number: 77–159566
ISBN 0–87663–148–0

Printed in Great Britain

Contents

The danger with acquiring a technique is that it can constrict, can make you think that's the way you have to do it; the lively part of it can be if it makes the way you would naturally dance more natural and extends what fits you.

MERCE CUNNINGHAM

There is a vitality, a life-force, an energy, a quickening that is translated through you into action and because there is only one of you in all of time, this expression is unique. And if you block it, it will never exist through any other medium and will be lost. The world will not have it.

MARTHA GRAHAM

Personality is a flimsy thing on which to build an art.

JOHN CAGE

Introduction

Experiment: almost everyone would agree it is essential; without it any art or science dies. But what, and how much? At this point background, preconceptions, context begin to dictate different answers.

What in fact is experimental dance? No definition will do unless it covers the extreme possibilities at either end of the artistic range. Like, for instance, the man in New York inside a cube of plastic sheeting, wearing no clothes but jumping energetically in and out of pools of paint. Or the white-costumed group in The Hague dancing with no apparent emotion to calm, gentle music in a changing context of square structures below, above or around them. It must include pure-dance works in the classical technique by George Balanchine and multi-media presentations by producers who never had a dance lesson in their lives. It must include work by composers, painters and sculptors who involve their work with dancing.

I see my brief as covering any theatrical or similar activity which tries to use dance in a new way or a new context. This does not set out to be a complete guide to the subject (any such attempt would soon be out of date) but an account and analysis of some of the many activities which have enlivened dance in our time and are likely to continue doing so for quite a while.

Some of these activities fall into no easily definable category. Others come within the spheres of ballet or modern dance, which can be equally experimental in their own ways, even though people deeply involved with either may find it difficult to see the point of what the other is trying to do.

The picture becomes clearer if you look back to a previous generation; for instance, to the early years of this century when Mikhail Fokine and Isadora Duncan were both in their prime, one trying to revitalize the classical tradition, the other trying to start a new tradition. Now, looking back, the similarities between them are even more striking than their differences. Each was concerned to find a way of using dance as a fresh and pliant expression of human emotion. Each, for inspiration, went back to older styles of art or took a new look at nature.

They and their contemporaries prepared the way for what is happening today; although this book is primarily about the present scene, it is worth while to look first at the background against which it developed. After that I shall try to make clear some of the general ideas underlying experiment in the dance today before going on to the discussion of individual creative artists which forms the main bulk of this book: describing what they are doing, also (as far as possible) why, and whenever practicable using their own words on the subject.

Part 1

THE PREDECESSORS

Isadora Duncan had everything against her. Brought up in a family of eccentrics, encouraged to display herself in genteel entertainments in drawing rooms, inclined to an emotionally and materially extravagant life, she could easily have been in reality what many of her contemporaries thought her: a dilettante enjoying a brief vogue. Yet even dancers who never saw her will today name her as their greatest inspiration.

You have only to look at drawings or photographs of Isadora to know that she was a great dancer. Why? One of her contemporaries, Ruth St Denis, put it that 'as she danced, she invoked in her audience every last ounce of poetry in them. She did not startle or plead; she evoked.' Another fellow-dancer, Helen Tamiris, confirms this view: 'At the finish, everyone was crying and I was crying too, although it took me many years to understand what she was doing—that she was living an action or an inner motivation and I was living with her.'

My own direct knowledge of her dancing is tiny and achieved not even at second but third or fourth hand. A pupil of Isadora's pupils, Julia Levien, gave two demonstration classes in London with a mixed collection of young dancers and amateurs. Even with such mainly untalented bodies she was able to convey something of the quality of movement and to show three or four of Isadora's dances: a Brahms waltz, a brief tragic entry, some fragments from Gluck's *Orpheus*. It was enough to prove what greatness must have been in the original.

Because of this greatness, Isadora Duncan was able to win acceptance for some revolutionary and invaluable ideas: that dancing could use great music, and that it could express serious themes, were perhaps the most important of them; but she also showed a free-flowing, lyrical way of moving and (as was necessary for this) established the right to wear free-flowing, unrestrictive clothes while dancing.

Her influence on later generations has been almost entirely as an inspiration: an example of the power of dance to move human feelings, and of the artist's right to claim complete freedom in finding his own way to achieve this. It was her contemporaries who codified and institutionalized modern dance. Is that a contradiction in terms? An alternative name for modern dance was 'the free dance'. How can free dance be taught and codified?

Ruth St Denis and her partner-husband Ted Shawn tried. After starting her career as a 'skirt dancer' with high kicks and splits, Miss St Denis was inspired (by a cigarette poster!) to invent dances which tried to present the spirit of the orient and, through this, religious themes. Independently of Isadora but at the same time she developed ideas of dancing barefoot and with unrestraining clothes or even none, and of using movement invented to express an idea instead of a set vocabulary of steps. But she found practical points about the use of breath and muscles which she could pass on to others, and she also wanted other dancers to develop her ideas of 'music visualizations' on a grand scale. So she and her husband started the Denishawn School from which came the next generation of American modern dancers.

The leaders of this generation, Doris Humphrey, Charles Weidman and Martha Graham, became outstanding mainly by reacting against everything they had been taught and inventing subjects, styles and approaches to music of their own. Miss Graham explained to me once:

I came late to Denishawn. They were already established as a company. We had ballet (not on point) and a fairly strict training. I realised soon that I had to find something to dance about. I could not just go around and be an attractive young girl on stage in a sari.
This does not mean that I don't treasure what I got from them, because I got from Denishawn an almost philosophic belief in dance as a means of communication. Miss St Denis was a didactic and very sincere and talented woman, but I realised that my way must go on a different way. So I left Denishawn and to tide over and earn some money I went into the Greenwich Village Follies as a soloist for two years. I did solos very reminiscent of Denishawn. Then, when that was over, I vowed I would not dance again until I could dance a different way.
I did not set out to be a rebel—I like comfort too much—but in a funny way you don't choose these things, they choose you, and then your life is increasingly not your own.
I taught what I knew, and developed myself for teaching— which is dangerous, but it was at a time when I suppose something was needed, and I had a bad enough temper and enough arrogance to work it out. I kept experimenting, and I hope to keep experimenting, because of the wonder of the human body and the magic of the spirit that is in each person.

Eventually the 'Graham technique' established itself as the most widely adopted programme of training available in modern dance, partly because of its originator's prestige and power as a performer and choreographer, partly because her analytical mind led to the formulation of a school capable of developing a dancer's muscles and mind from scratch in a logical way. Far from imposing a standard style on those who study it, this technical method has shown itself capable of adaptation in creative hands to widely varying purposes.

Concurrently with the establishing of contemporary dance (as Graham prefers to call it) in America, a modern dance movement flourished in Europe, primarily in Germany. Rudolf von Laban (best known now as the inventor of one of the most widely adopted systems of movement notation) was a key figure. His attempt to establish the principles of theatrical movement with the aid of psychological, geometrical and philosophical analysis remained, perhaps inevitably, somewhat arid, but attracted enthusiastic disciples. His was an intellectual approach in contrast to the emotional approach of Duncan and St Denis; he used, for instance, an icosahedron, a structure of metal strips making a hollow model with twenty equal triangular faces, to define various possibilities of reach, inclination and direction. Into a second-hand copy I bought of one of Laban's textbooks, a former owner has stuck photographs of a naked young woman inside this structure solemnly delineating some possible positions, each with its own coded description. Laban's own creative work for giant 'movement choirs' has disappeared almost without trace, but two of his pupils have left their mark on the dance tradition.

One of these was Mary Wigman, whose style was dark, heavy and intense, a demonic response to outside influences. She experimented in dances performed in silence, or with only a rhythmic accompaniment; and through schools in Dresden, Leipzig, Berlin and New York she passed on some of her ideas to a generation of pupils.

Kurt Jooss, by contrast, used a formidable theatrical instinct first to breathe some life into Laban's dry theories, then to move away from them to something more free. His earliest works reveal the obsession with masks and concealing costumes common in the 1920s, but in *The Green Table* he found an indignant social message (about war and politics) which inspired him to a vivid, poster-art dance of death. Apart from thus creating the first (and, for nearly thirty years thereafter, the last) European masterwork of modern dance, Jooss was also important for showing in his later productions a growing influence of other dance forms, even including ballet, and thus lending respectability to the reconciliation of two traditions previously thought incompatible.

But to go back: when Isadora Duncan was in Russia she inspired the young Mikhail Fokine to new faith in the programme for reforming classical ballet which he was already preparing. This in turn helped lead to the founding of Diaghilev's Russian Ballet and the enlistment of major European composers and painters to assist the rebirth of ballet as a major art form. No need here to repeat the familiar story of Diaghilev's many experiments in changing ballet; but his one-time rivals, the Ballets Suédois founded by Rolf de Maré, deserve mention, because together with some folklore elements they also included a good deal of avant-garde experimentation.

Would it really be possible even today, for instance, to devise a work more outrageous than *Relâche* (No Performance)? Satie's music was cheerfully irreverent; Picabia decorated one scene with hundreds of hanging discs, the other with messages such as 'Ceux qui ne sont pas contents sont autorisés à f... le camp' and 'Il y en a qui préfèrent les ballets de l'Opéra, les pauvres imbéciles'.

Dancers came up from the auditorium to take part in Borlin's choreography, men stripped off their evening dress on stage to reveal long white fleshings, a fireman stood there pouring water from one bucket to another. There was a film, too, by René Clair, which included sequences such as a huntsman who succeeds in reaching an egg dancing on a jet of water; from the egg issues a pigeon which settles on a man's hat; the huntsman shoots at it and kills the man.

Quite a lot of today's experimentation was foreshadowed or even forestalled by *Relâche*; and that was in 1924. This was a consciously revolutionary work (designed, Picabia said, to put 'a good many kicks up a good many backsides'); but a point I want to make is that even so apparently quiet and formal a ballet as Fokine's *Les Sylphides*, fifteen years earlier, was in its way also experimental—maybe even revolutionary, in showing a new form for a plotless but sustained choreographic work. And also that, although to their contemporaries Fokine and Isadora Duncan looked very different, *Les Sylphides*—with its use of serious music by Chopin, its drawing of inspiration mainly from that music rather than predetermined set forms, its gentle lyricism and its free use of the arms—had a lot in common with what the revolutionary Isadora was doing at the same time.

WHERE AND WHEN

Experiment is most likely to be found where some form of dance is already well established. If you are trying to start activity where none existed before, either you are likely to model your work after traditional examples, or else the experiments you try will probably be of limited interest and success for lack of a fixed starting point. When there is plenty of traditional dance to revolt against, plus a creative atmosphere, experiment stands most chance of succeeding.

The creative atmosphere is partly a matter of the general artistic scene at the time, partly of a specific place or group concerned with creation. Take, for instance, one of the most famous centres of the avant-garde in dance, Judson Church in New York. This pseudo-Florentine building, complete with campanile, stands in Greenwich Village, amid a congregation not exactly renowned for orthodoxy in religion or anything else. Clive Barnes wrote of it that 'quite a lot of good, bad and indifferent work is going on, with most of it naturally indifferent. However, over all of it, even the most appalling, there is a sort of seriousness, a total belief in the value of what is being created.'

In an article in the *Village Voice*, Jill Johnston described the beginnings: 'Nobody set out to "make" a movement. The dancers and non-dancers who had been studying composition with Robert Dunn at Merce Cunningham's studio decided they needed a place to perform, and they found the church. Such a consolidation, vital as it may be, contains the seeds of its death in the increasing independence of its members.' One of the original participants, Judith Dunn, defined the value of the venture:

The Judson Church, by making a place for dance and its continuous performance, has uniquely provided that thing which without exception dancers must have . . . It was and still is opportunity.
Opportunity for continuous performance and radical, uncensored experimentation on all levels of production. Each concert, be it group or individual, can (and does) shape itself to the interests and needs of its creators. The theater, playing area, what have you, is literally made each time anew, theater and dance tradition exists, there is no need to question on that level. It was. However, because of the moment, the uncluttered space, the particular group maybe, the opportunity definitely and the freedom from financial concern (there simply was no money, this was accepted as a spur to invention rather than a handicap), the traditions as they existed in the formal sense were bypassed. This bypassing has allowed for a diversity in the approach to work and for radical experimentation as well as the inclusion as performers and choreographers of those who in the traditional sense would not be considered dancers. In view of this and in spite of the popularity certain aspects of the work have gained, I feel that the Judson Dance Theater is not a 'group', is more than a 'movement' and more than any one person's view of its products . . .
The people in the Dance Theater were each involved in something of their own, something special; and also the Dance Theater was happening at a time when everyone was willing to cooperate. That was really one of the unique aspects about it. For some reason, probably it had to do with the fact that there had been these classes, there were really 30 people who were willing to cooperate, to be in each other's pieces, to give themselves to certain technical tasks—I stage-managed the first program, for example, and others, and I loved doing it, it was really marvelous to participate in all the aspects—you'd be dancing one minute and the next minute you'd be stringing up a light or something.

Another thing that happened at Judson was that painters and sculptors began to be involved with dance, not only as designers but as producers and performers. Alex Hay, Robert Morris and Robert Rauschenberg were among those taking part. At a concert given by the group in State University College, New Paltz, New York, in January 1964, a programme note declared that 'In the curious way in which the art world changes, painters have made inroads into theatrical performances. Artists find that there are no unacceptable sources for material. The repertoire of Judson Dance

Theater reflects the latest of this recent tendency to allow freer play. Dancers, mixed with painters on the stage, point out how there is another quality to bodies than just the arrived-at differences dancers have discovered in themselves—there is the whole look of the body, which knows a lot on its own and, whether "trained" or not, relays much of its history with action.'

The point about a place like Judson is that by offering opportunities for performance it encourages cross-fertilization of ideas among those who use these opportunities; thus in more senses than one, things happen which would not otherwise have happened. Something similar can happen within any continuing venture, given the right circumstances. Both Hans van Manen and Glen Tetley, for instance, had shown themselves inclined to experimental forms and attitudes before they took joint charge of the artistic policies of Netherlands Dance Theatre, but it was not until they came together in this way that they followed some of their ideas to more extreme ends: involving filmed sequences with live dancers, for instance; producing *Mutations* with its nude sequences, or inviting Peter Dockley to stage an event involving the dancers, *Never Never Land*. Likewise, a simple decision to adopt a different, more consciously creative policy led within Ballet Rambert to an accelerating movement towards greater company participation in policy and production, the adoption of a different style, the trying of new subjects and forms. Experiment is sometimes hard to start, but once started it is often difficult to stop until its logical development is completed and it stops itself because there is nothing left to do.

This can be true of buildings as well as organizations. Once a building is known to be available for activity of a certain kind, people interested in providing that activity will make their way to it. The example of Judson Church is borne out by what happened in London when first the Arts Laboratory was opened in a former nail factory in Drury Lane, offering a small informal stage which attracted groups from Holland or even further afield as well as local ones; and then by the experience of The Place, founded (in a former army drill hall) primarily as a home for the London Contemporary Dance Theatre and School. The availability of its studio theatre and an interested audience led to visits by companies from Poland, Sweden, Israel, even the Argentine; and cumulatively this helped further to develop the building's reputation, and thus also its potential, for a certain kind of experiment.

Not that a theatre is necessary for dance activity. A disused armoury or railway shed, a circus ring or sports palace, the basement of an art gallery—these are just some of the places which have made a place for dance from time to time. Merce Cunningham has staged several events in museums, selecting works (or parts of works) from his repertory according to the available space. He has also shown some of his works in basketball courts, using all or part of different dances, crossing dances where possible and using as much of the court as would work with a given dance or dances. Obviously, dance in these circumstances can easily become very different from dance in a conventional theatre, and thus a further element of change or experiment enters.

THE NEW MUSIC FOR DANCE

As recently as 1958 it was possible for Humphrey Searle, a reputable composer (a former member, incidentally, of the Sadler's Wells Ballet Advisory Panel) to write that good ballet music 'must have rhythm and colour; melody, though desirable, is not so completely essential . . . It is best if the music is in short self-contained sections, each of which can be fitted to an individual dance: or if the ballet is based on a longer continuous work, such as a symphonic poem for instance, it should contain a large number of short episodes or changes of mood which can be paralleled in the choreography.'

Twelve years later, the scores used for new productions by the Royal Ballet during 1970 included one in which the musicians had to speak their names, the names of their instruments and that of the orchestra; one specially composed for electronic tape; one combining electronic and orchestral elements; and one to a score by Stockhausen which substitutes instructions to the musicians for the more conventional system of musical notation, then electronically transforms the sounds they make. And that is the conservative, traditionalist Royal Ballet.

Music has changed a lot, and because of this, the way dancers make use of it has changed too. The old idea was that the composer should produce 'danceable rhythms' which would inspire the choreographer. With much modern music, the choreographer has to invent his own rhythms; even while using music, the point of independence has been reached, towards which some previously aspired by trying to do without music altogether.

Silence rarely works. David Lichine tried it with *La Création*, although I am not entirely sure that the choreography was created without benefit of music, since Lichine had previously mounted a ballet on the same or a similar theme in South America, using Franck's *Symphonic Variations*, and his silent ballet was the right length, and had the changes of mood or action at about the right places, to have fitted reasonably easily to that music. Jerome Robbins's silent ballet *Moves* was originally rehearsed to a score which was eventually thought unsuitable. The effect of such ballets danced in silence in a repertory otherwise making ordinary use of music was to shame into stillness the coughers and paper-rustlers who inhabit any audience, and to compel an intensity of concentration well above the average. It seems unlikely however that this would work other than as a rare exception.

On the other hand, there is no need for the choreographer to use music as a crutch. Probably the first example of using music purely as an accompaniment, with the dance pursuing its quite independent way, is Nijinsky's *L'Après-midi d'un Faune*, where the Debussy music and the Bakst designs were about equally important in setting a mood and about equally irrelevant to the movements being performed by the dancers, except that the total length of the action was determined by that of the music. Nijinsky was a pioneer who had no followers for many years. One of the first postwar examples of a similar approach was *Le Jeune Homme et la Mort*, designated on the programme as having 'danse, décor et costumes racontés par Jean Cocteau' to the choreographer, designers and dancers, and specified 'Une musique de Bach accompagnera les danses'. The work was actually rehearsed to jazz music and the Bach passacaglia added only at the last minute.

Nevertheless, even if a choreographer nowadays is far less likely to work to the beat of the music, he will still pay attention to general suitability, and sometimes to far more than this. Rudi van Dantzig, who prefers to use electronic scores (partly through temperamental inclination, partly because they are always the same, whereas a ballet with an orchestral score normally has to be rehearsed to a misleading piano accompaniment) told me that with a commissioned score, such as the one by Jan Boerman for *The Ropes of Time*, he gives the composer an outline of the action he intends, but is likely to modify that action on receiving the completed score, because the music puts fresh ideas, or variants of old ideas, into his mind.

This is not the place for a detailed account of the development of music in this century, either the new techniques of composition for conventional instruments (serialism, etc.), or the use of recorded natural sounds other than those of these instruments (musique concrète) or of sounds produced entirely with the aid of an electronic tape in a studio. But the extent to which composition has changed from the old forms is indicated by, for instance, this sleeve note by Stockhausen for a recording of his *Kontakte* (used by Glen Tetley for his ballet *Ziggurat*):

The electronic sounds were produced by means of an impulse generator (the speed of the impulses can be continuously varied between 16 and $\frac{1}{16}$ impulses per second, and the duration of the impulses between $\frac{1}{10000}$ and $\frac{9}{10}$ of a second.) A 'tunable indicator amplifier' (as a relatively narrow filter with continuously variable band-width and correspondingly varied durations of decay) and an adjustable band-filter were also used. For a few sound-events, sinus-wave generators and a square-wave generator were employed. Most of the sounds, sound-noises or noises were made by various accelerations of rhythmic sequences of impulses. For certain sounds, an echo-sheet with continuously variable echo durations was used.

The applicability of the new music to dancing varies according to the choreographer's intentions and methods of work. At least two avant-garde composers who have written specially for dancing have expressed clear views on the subject. Bernd Alois Zimmermann, whose works include *Présence*, an outstanding success in John Cranko's staging for his Stuttgart company, pointed out that 'The music of the classical ballet articulates time by marking the emphases of the beat and, so to speak, "putting before the dancer's eyes" the measured time of the music, which coincides with that of the motion. Here the music without doubt has an auxiliary or serving function, and indeed the classical pieces of ballet music are synchronizations of the processes of motion prescribed by the ballet canon; they are actually assessed by the degree to which they can "carry" the dancer.'

Against this, he suggested that 'for the ballet of the future we must demand (so far as it is not already to hand) a music that evolves musical structures in such a fashion that it enables the dancer in turn to establish a counterpoint to these through dancing structures. In this I see the purest form of ballet music. Of course the invention of absolute musical structures without regard to their dancing counterpoint is not enough. Instead, the composer must leave space for the choreographer to evolve dancing structures.'

What concerned Zimmermann was 'a basal reciprocal interpenetration of ballet and music structures' and he considered that 'the ballet of the future will be a very complex one. All elements of the theatre of movement, including film, sound, speech, electronic music, must be mobilized into one great space–time structure, whose arrangement will be constituted by music as the most general form of temporal order.'

Against this is the view of John Cage, who wrote in explanation of some of his performances with Merce Cunningham and Dance Company that:

Though some of the dances and music are easily enjoyed, others are perplexing to certain people, for they do not unfold along conventional lines. For one thing, there is an independence of the music and dance, which, if one closely observes, is present also in the seemingly usual works. This independence follows from Mr Cunningham's faith, which I share, that the support of the dance is not to be found in the music but in the dancer himself, on his own two legs, that is, and occasionally on a single one. Likewise the music sometimes consists of single sounds or groups of sounds which are not supported by harmonies but resound within a space of silence. From this independence of music and dance a rhythm results which is not that of horses' hoofs or other regular beats but which reminds us of a multiplicity of events in time and space—stars, for instance, in the sky, or activities on earth viewed from the air.

B

Both Zimmermann and Cage want the complex pattern, but Zimmermann saw it evolving through highly organized inter- actions, Cage from simultaneity of disparate activities. Cage had come into close concern with dance for purely practical reasons. As a student he became aware of his teacher's unhappiness 'in face of the fact that his music was rarely performed. I too had experienced difficulty in arranging performances of my own compositions, so I determined to consider a piece of music only half done when I completed a manuscript. It was my responsibility to finish it by getting it played. It was evident that musicians interested in new music were rare. It was equally evident that modern dancers were grateful for any sounds or noises that could be produced for their recitals.' He first met Cunningham as a student, a very remarkable one, in 1937; later encouraged him to give programmes of his own dances and has worked with him since 1943.

Cage has been not only a leading practitioner but the principal theorist of the new music. He points out in his book *Silence* how much modern music owes to the development of processes during World War II for magnetically recording sounds. First used for high-fidelity recording, this magnetic tape was used first in France with the work of Pierre Schaeffer, later in the USA, Germany, Italy, Japan and elsewhere for the actual composition of music that would not be practicable otherwise. Cage argues that scales, modes, theories of counterpoint and harmony, etc., are needed when composing for old instruments, but 'in mathematical terms these all concern discrete steps. They resemble walking—in the case of pitches, on steppingstones twelve in number. This cautious stepping is not characteristic of the possibilities of magnetic tape, which is revealing to us that musical action or existence can occur at any point or along any line or curve or what have you in total sound-space.'

To take advantage of these possibilities involves being willing to change one's habits radically, just as is the case also with other developments: television, for instance, or aircraft. New music needs 'new listening . . . attention to the activity of sounds'.

I mentioned the practical consideration which led Cage to involve his music with dancing. There is a reciprocal practical benefit; for many people, it is a lot easier to become acquainted with unfamiliar music in the theatre when the eye is also active, taking in new experiences. When the relationship of choreography and music is close, the one can help clarify the other; but even when this is not the case, the circumstance of attentiveness to a visual stimulus seems to facilitate aural attentiveness also, and vice versa. So experimental music and experimental dance go naturally together, help each other—and in consequence perhaps spur each other on to fresh experiment.

ABOUT FORM AND CONTENT

The time is probably approaching when nobody will dream of writing an ordinary book about ballet. Ideally, any ballet criticism is related to an actual performance. So far, if the reader has not been present at the same performance as the author, the latter has had to do his best to describe what he saw, sometimes with the aid of photographs, before commenting on it. How much better to have some kind of audio-video-cassette, either to replace or supplement the printed word, so that the author can say 'Look!' and comment on the work while the reader sees on a screen just what he is referring to.

One consequence of books about ballet is that people tend to think the essence of a work can be extracted and set down on paper. A title like *The Complete Book of Ballets* is given to what its author, Cyril Beaumont, defines as 'a collection of the stories of the principal ballets of the nineteenth and twentieth centuries'. That author was conscientious enough to be inconsistent and try, wherever possible, to give some description also of the choreography and some of the outstanding individual performances, but the basis of his approach is inevitably that the story is the most important element. Even a choreographer like Balanchine lends his weight to the view with the similar volume *Balanchine's Complete Stories of the Great Ballets*, although in the preface he declares that his own ballets are difficult to describe and that the book is 'merely trying to prepare the reader for a theatrical experience'.

The fact is that the story of a ballet is rarely its most important element, and often the least important. This can be true even of works with a complicated plot difficult to set down on paper: in fact it is especially likely to be true in such circumstances because such 'stories' probably indicate a lack of care for plausibility on the part of the original creators.

During the present century two things have happened to ballet plots. First, the number of ballets without a plot at all has increased; *Les Sylphides* was once a rarity but is now a norm. Secondly, the way of telling the story has changed a lot in recent years. I say 'story' but often this is the wrong word. A ballet may have some clear intellectual content without having a narrative plot in the old sense. A choreographer who has often worked on these lines is John Cranko. His *Présence* involves three archetypal characters from literature: Molly Bloom, Don Quixote and Ubu Roi, representing the sensual, brutal and idealistic aspects of human nature; or in psychological terms id, ego and super-ego. On the surface this ballet is a charade with many comic elements, including an operation on Molly during which she sings an operatic coloratura aria while unlikely objects are extracted from her stomach, and another scene in which she gradually disappears into the embraces of an amorous sofa. The mimed action is interspersed with dance passages for which the characters leave off their identifying costumes, wearing just an initial on their leotards. As a narrative, it is literally indescribable in terms which would make coherent literary sense; but as a ballet about sex, power and idealism it makes perfect sense.

Many modern dance choreographers have gone further than this in presenting their themes in terms which the spectator must appreciate directly, from the dance and music images, rather than translating them first into literary images. Others go further still, to the point where the content of the dance is not specified at all by the creator. John Cage states quite categorically about the work of Cunningham and himself:

We are not, in these dances and music, saying something. We are simple-minded enough to think that if we were saying something we would use words. We are rather doing something. The meaning of what we do is determined by each one who sees and hears it. . . .
There are no stories and no psychological problems. There is simply an activity of movement, sound and light. The costumes are all simple in order that you many see the movement.
The movement is the movement of the body. It is here that Mr Cunningham focuses his choreographic attention, not on the facial muscles. In daily life people customarily observe faces and hand gestures, translating what they see into psychological terms. Here, however, we are in the presence of a dance which utilizes the entire body, requiring for its enjoyment the use of your faculty of kinesthetic sympathy. It is this faculty we employ when, seeing the flight of birds, we ourselves, by identification, fly up, glide and soar.
The activity of movement, sound, and light, we believe, is expressive, but what it expresses is determined by each one of you—who is right, as Pirandello's title has it, if he thinks he is. The novelty of our work derives therefore from our having moved away from simply private human concerns towards the world of nature and society of which all of us are a part.

The description could give the impression that there is no dramatic incident in the resulting works. Far from it. In *Place*, for example, Cunningham remains an aloof, focal figure while others move, sometimes in quick bursts of frenzied energy, sometimes in sculptural groups which edge their way almost imperceptibly across the performing area. From a screen, covering the upper half of the back of the stage, hang newspapers and grids of slatted wood, suggesting a constricting, unamiable urban environment. Cunningham alone seems to exercise some control over this environment; he moves about a little heap of objects on which a light appears. But at the end, alone again, he walks calmly across the stage, bends down and suddenly forces himself into a huge plastic bag with movements of such fierce desperation that they jerk him across the stage again and right out of sight under the hanging objects; his disappearance is like an orgasm or a death. To watch, this work has a remarkable fascination, and although its drama cannot be explained in rational terms, its effect is real and powerful.

Yet only a few years before Cunningham made *Place*, Antony Tudor had created *Pillar of Fire*, the first (and so far still the best) psychological ballet, in which the action is gradually seen to take place within the mind of the heroine. This is achieved by gradually changing from a realistic to an abstract setting while the dance action shows a more and more distorted view of events. Cunningham aimed at a non-specific situation, Tudor at a very specific one which would enable him to show not merely what happened, but why and how it affected his characters. They had one thing in common: both by their experiments enlarged the expressive scope of the dance.

Once it had been accepted that the story was no longer the key element in a ballet's structure, far greater freedom of form became possible. This applies to those works which retain a plot as well as to those which abandon it. At one time for instance, if you were telling a story in dancing it was more or less obligatory to begin at the beginning and go on to the end, just as in the normal novel. But even the novel has been affected by the process of fragmentation which occurred in most arts during the present century, and dancing far more so. In fact nowadays dance creators are far more likely to be influenced by the cinema than by literature anyway. The plot of Kenneth MacMillan's ballet *The Invitation* is based on a combination of incidents from two novels, but only indirectly: MacMillan saw the filmed versions of these novels and took his inspiration from those.

In the changed approach to narrative, the nature of the plots chosen for dancing has also played a part in changing the form adopted. A nineteenth-century mythological ballet would use its plot partly for its own poetic implications, partly as a convenient line on which to peg a number of dances either purely decorative or expressing certain formalized emotions. When someone like Martha Graham takes a mythological subject today, her interest is a different one: 'People say I've used the myths too much. The only reason I have used them is that they express the terror, the beauty and the will to live of people over thousands of years.'

The later development of Graham's work, as she invented increasingly less active roles for herself, helped to emphasize another tendency that had already been present in her work, namely a free use of time sequences, not necessarily consecutive but with the same effect of switching from one time to another (with simultaneity, flashback and so on) as film-makers allow themselves. There are instances when time scarcely matters at all: the comparatively early *Appalachian Spring* can be seen as the events of an evening, but it is easy (perhaps easier) to accept them as occurring in a timeless limbo, a distillation of many incidents into one evocation of a place and its inhabitants.

I am citing Graham because her work is widely known and influential, but the process was by no means confined to her. Antony Tudor's *Dim Lustre* for instance is based entirely on the memories evoked in a dancing couple by a kiss, a touch on the shoulder, a perfume, a white tie, so that present and past alternate until the couple realize that there is no future for them together. Once a startling novelty, this sort of construction would now be accepted as perfectly straightforward.

Form and structure of dance works have changed in another direction too. Ballet, drama and other arts, formerly self-sufficient and self-contained, are now often combined in various ways. First the ideal was 'total theatre'—a bit of everything, acting, singing, dancing, each done by different specialists. More recently the different elements are likely to be linked more intimately.

On the one hand you have choreographers introducing other elements into their dance-works: films in Kenneth MacMillan's *Anastasia* for instance, or in the *Mutations* which Glen Tetley and Hans van Manen did jointly; singing in Van Manen's *Solo for Voice 1*; speech in Alwin Nikolais's *Tower*. At the same time you have people with other specialities approaching a similar result from another direction: apart from the painters and sculptors previously mentioned and other outsiders discussed in detail later, there have been examples such as the lavish production of *Rabelais* mounted (first in Paris, later on an international tour) by Jean-Louis Barrault in which the actors danced and the dancers acted, so that the whole cast were involved in the whole action.

Often two media are inextricably linked in one work. In *Duet for One* (originally called *Blossom*) Beverley Schmidt danced both in a film directed by Roberts Blossom and on stage in front of the screen. *Prune, Flat* by Robert Whitman used films of fruit and other objects, also of dancers, and the same dancers live on stage, to contrast reality and illusion. Art Bauman's *Dialog* used films of himself running up and down the corridors and escalators of a bleak office building to supplement his own dancing on stage and convey the emptiness of material achievement.

A slightly different relationship between two media is that of film or television adaptation of a dance-work, which can often completely reinterpret the original. The Czech director Petr Weigl made a largely abstract *Pas de Quatre* based on themes from *Swan Lake* in which one dancer played both Odette and Odile, another both Siegfried and Rothbart, all four being shown at once by trick photography, and the whole providing a commentary on the relationship of the characters in the stage ballet. Alwin Nikolais's *Totem* has been adapted by Ed Emshwiller into a semi-abstract film with many effects of distortion, duplication or substitution to enhance its mystic symbolism. The German television producer Manfred Gräter made a programme *2 × Moments* about Rudi van Dantzig's stage ballet *Moments*. He explained that he had been very impressed by the ballet at its Amsterdam première 'and immediately felt the necessity to preserve this work for TV—not so much because of a special suitability for the medium, but rather because of my collector's passion. When, later on, Klaus Lindemann, the director I had commissioned, explained to me his very extravagant TV concept, I at once visualized a completely embarrassed and desperate Rudi van Dantzig, a new choreographic victim on the altar of TV. To guard against this, I had the idea of combining destruction and reparation, namely by producing a second version of *Moments* which seemed more likely to do justice to the intentions of the choreographer.' Thus *Moments* was produced twice, in a straightforward version exactly as set by the choreographer, and also in an experimental version 'which occasionally interfered with the basic choreography for the benefit of its visualisation suited to the screen'. A third team made a documentary film about both productions, with the choreographer commenting on his work and on the two directors. 'Thus simultaneously illustrative material was provided for the question, hitherto only theoretically discussed, of how far it is sensible and desirable to manipulate the original choreography for the dimension and dramaturgy of the TV picture.'

THE OUTSIDERS

Now that dance is no longer a coherent and organized world, stiff with tradition, it is possible for people with no dance training to approach it from different directions and contribute something of their own.

For instance, Taller de Montevideo, a group of six young people from Uruguay who were originally active in kinetic art, but later took the logical step of involving dancers with their work. One such event was *Chronus III* which they presented as part of the 'Explorations' series given to mark the opening of The Place as a dance centre in London. For this, they filled the centre of a studio with a structure comprising a collection of white rostrums, with various planes and levels from which emerged a series of white verticals. The dancers moved about this structure, forming different relationships and formal compositions with its parts, while the look of the structure itself was constantly changed by the use of lighting (occasionally coloured, with dramatic effect, but usually white in different patterns and degrees). Pulsating sound added another effect, and the spectators were expected to move about, so that they saw an ever-changing kaleidoscopic vision of these different elements. This group also tried to involve the public in a kind of art event by scattering structures along a footway (in a street or park) so that the pedestrians had either to move them or go round about: a kind of do-it-yourself dance on the simplest possible level.

Most of the outsiders overlapping into dance come from the visual arts, painting or sculpture, but other disciplines may lead the same way. Some mimes, for instance, find themselves in effect evolving towards a kind of dance. The Polish mime Henryk Tomaszewski not only presents big movement-spectacles with his own company but has staged works also for classical ballet companies in Holland and Denmark.

Holland has also produced more than one group of mimes who, to a greater extent than Tomaszewski, have broken down the barriers between traditional mime and dance. Classic mime imitates natural gestures to represent an activity or tell a story. These groups instead have orchestrated everyday movements into patterns in the same way that ballet orchestrates steps into patterns. One such was Will Spoor's mime group. A typical programme began with *Bugs' Counterpoint*. You cannot really imitate a bug in the way you can imitate a man; you can only represent him by jumping, rolling, crouching or whatever. So the three grey-wrapped figures who performed this piece had a wonderful time representing footloose and amorous bugs. In *Cardboard Column Canon* the performers were completely wrapped in tall columns of rolled corrugated paper, so that they were invisible except for a hand which came over the top of a column to wave soap bubbles in the air or drop a banana skin. The point about this piece was that it made the watcher intent for every tiny movement and forced him to deduce a larger movement from the small gesture seen.

Another of Spoor's works was called *Penis Invention*. Two men had enormous truncheons strapped to their bellies. These waved to and fro as the men moved about in a maze of corrugated paper which left them visible from the hips up. Eventually the pair met each other face to face and fought a duel with their phalluses, breaking off only when a girl entered and joined them. She produced two small fireworks which she stuck, one in the end of each of these wooden erections, then ignited them so that the piece ended in a discharge of pretty sparks.

The Bewth mime group from Holland worked on similar principles to Spoor, except that he used a stage and thus showed his pieces as essentially theatrical, while they did theirs in the middle of a room with the audience all round the walls. Their activities had no narrative content at all, although a piece might be built, for instance, on the contrast between a certain number of pleasant things like blowing bubbles and a certain number of related but unpleasant things, like blowing whistles. Purely decorative elements were introduced, like all the cast putting on coloured socks, and some things seemed intended as much for the sound element as the visual: a boy sitting down, for instance, and chomping noisily away at a cucumber and an apple. All this was much more like an exceptionally casual dance event than mime; in fact their finale was a dance in which some of the audience were persuaded to join.

A different way into dance was that followed by Geoff Moore. He was at art school and began working in the evenings as a stage hand at the local theatre simply to earn pocket-money. Here he saw plays, opera and ballet, and says, 'I was fascinated by the dancing, as it seemed that there was the basis of a lot of the things I wanted to do.' Yet he found that 'it was not the works that impressed me so much as the process; what could be done in, say, the extremity of a class, or just someone warming up, the sheer visual and physical intensity . . . I used to watch a lot of rehearsals and I found that the whole rehearsal process was more stimulating than the actual works, it seemed to contain the guts of the matter which became dissipated when it came to the way the language was applied.'

Moore's approach to dancing came from the juxtaposition of this stimulus and the ideas he was developing from his formal studies, in terms of visual awareness and organic structures. He developed an interest in 'a derangement of elements' which worked in terms of painting, collages and sculpture, and wanted to apply the same process to dance and theatre.

His first attempts were purely spatial designs, sculptural arrangements of figures in space with sound and other elements. Next he worked on movement relating one figure to another and to a musical basis, first with students and then with people who had a little dance training. From this he went on to add other elements: slide projections which would relate (often ironically) to the physical action; a sound track which would add a further level of comment; and eventually the introduction of some speech by the performers.

The intention was to 'develop a multi-levelled event where people could be surprised, hopefully, by spontaneous reactions, and that the audience wouldn't get only what they had become conditioned to get, but that it would be stimulating in terms of extending things. If a particular discipline or a particular convention was at some point broken through and then returned to, what might result would be some sort of an illumination.'

In one section of Moore's *Quartet* the process worked like this. Two couples danced in short phrases, passing the impetus from one pair to the other with the muttered word 'change'. Meanwhile the soundtrack carried three separate narrations, given alternately in short snatches with often ironic juxtapositions. One voice told a campus love story; another discussed the nature of eroticism, its place in marriage and the possible origin of various sexual customs; a third read a newspaper account of the inquest on a teenage girl who killed herself after her husband left her with their young baby. The cutting from one theme to another was like the cutting from one image to another in a film; each made more point by contrast. In this instance, however, there was also the additional visual counterpoint of the dancers entwined, clambering over each other, moving slowly around.

From this stage, Moore went on to create a work for the Ballet Rambert, *Remembered Motion*, this time involving highly trained professional dancers in a context of an analysis of a girl's past sexual and emotional hang-ups, with a soundtrack of voices discussing the past, sometimes emotionally, sometimes rationally, and with the girl herself, past and present, represented simultaneously by two different dancers.

The next stage either had to be an advance into organized ballet (and presumably the acquisition of some dance training himself to be able to know and take advantage of the dancers' potentialities) or a sidestep. Moore chose the latter, forming his own group Moving Being with actors, dancers and technicians, to present multi-media productions of increasing complexity. In all his programmes, dance remained an essential element: either in short, selfcontained dance pieces as part of a mixed programme, or as an element in long works. The structure of his works has become increasingly intellectual, even didactic, but the use of visual elements deriving from pop, vaudeville, classic ballet, advertising and many other sources has sustained interest at the level both of entertainment and of formal construction.

Another group using dance as one of many composite elements in their work is the TSE company which started in Buenos Aires but is now based in Paris. Whereas Moore aims at a multi-media presentation, TSE are primarily concerned with presenting a dramatic spectacle more like a play but in a stylized form with the use of music, dance and designs. In *Dracula*, the familiar story was told in a style based on strip cartoons. Wearing fantastic costumes, one or two characters entered at a time, spoke a few words, and froze into artificial poses while a pop score accompanied the action. All the movement was very stilted, designed to give a two-dimensional effect; the verbal delivery was equally artificial. In *Goddess*, the movie-heroine title part (based on Maria Felix, one of the great cinema stars of Spanish-speaking South America) was played by a man balanced on enormous platform soles, accompanied everywhere by two acolytes. These productions were largely ignored by people connected with drama but admired by many whose activity was dance; Peter Darrell for one was greatly influenced by them in the conception of his *Herodias* which included a spoken poem (by Mallarmé) and very elaborate costumes and make-up. But both the TSE company and Geoff Moore have presented works in which some of the dancers appeared without any costumes.

Dancing without clothes is nothing new. Duncan and St Denis both appeared in scanty draperies, their contemporary Maud Allen was notorious for her dance as Salome and German or American books of dance photographs in the early years of this century show a good many dancers in abbreviated garments or none at all.

Nudity has been used several times lately in dance, chiefly for its shock effect. Ann Halprin, for instance, in *Parades and Changes*, had the young and good-looking cast take off all their clothes at the beginning, then put them on, then take them off again, during which time some got out of phase with the others, but eventually all ended stark naked, frolicking in piles of brown paper which they tore, crumpled and bundled up before all jumping into the empty orchestra pit. Don McDonagh, reviewing it, wrote that 'it was sweet and innocent, and as a brochure for nudity effective, but lacked the drawing power to make one want to see it again, except of course for prurient reasons'.

Usually, discussions of naked dancers assume that the prurient reasons do not exist (unless of course they are aiming to have the nakedness banned). This seems rather insulting. Dancers generally have well-formed, attractive bodies, and to pretend that there is no sexual interest at all in seeing one without clothes does little credit to watcher or watched. On the other hand, with any serious use of public nudity, prurience is likely to take a secondary place to other interests—if the piece is good enough.

When Joe Schlichter danced his *Cube* at The Bridge in New York in 1966, he entered the plastic cube with blue paint already dripping from his hair and threw himself so forcefully against one wall that he bounced off and hit the ground hard. Repeating this process and generally throwing himself about within the walls of plastic sheeting, he fell repeatedly in pools of red and white paint until his body was covered, patriotically if not very concealingly, in dripping red, white and blue. If he had worn clothes, or even tights, the effect of this would have been very different from his actual naked state. This was plainly a non-sexual use of nudity in dancing (provided, that is, that you accept his activity as dancing. If it isn't, what is it?).

At the other extreme are the offerings of strip club touts: 'Eighteen lovely girls—they're naked and they dance.' (I must confess I have always been intrigued by the Soho strip club from which I heard issuing one day the sound of the *Nutcracker* pas de deux.)

In between are those dances which use nudity for a relevant artistic purpose. In *Window*, Geoff Moore had a couple naked at the end to suggest their innocence in contrast with the black-swathed rest of the cast. Nudity in this circumstance does in fact look more innocent than semi-nudity; another of Moore's pieces had a girl wearing semi-transparent white body-tights and nothing else, which looked vaguely indecent.

Innocent, yes; unsensuous, no. Even clothed, the dancer's body is an object of sensuous interest. But even when clothed, dancing is an energetic activity and it is not unknown for a shoulderstrap to break or a costume to become more revealing than was intended. I think most people if honest would admit that this can be a lot more distracting than complete and planned nudity. What you are not meant to see is generally more fascinating than what you are.

The real point is, I think, that everything depends on the purpose of the creator and performer. If there is a genuine reason for appearing nude it will probably look right. It will also probably (human nature being what it is) help the box office. But if there is no real reason for it, the effect is likely to embarrass as many people as it gratifies.

Part 2

ASPIRING TO THE STATE OF MUSIC—
FYODOR LOPUKHOV TO GEORGE BALANCHINE

The mid-1920s were a time of much innovation and invention in the classical ballet. At the one extreme you have in 1923 the première by the Diaghilev Ballet of Nijinska's *Les Noces*, the first and still the best staging of Stravinsky's great choral and percussion score based on Russian peasant weddings. Both Nijinska and the designer Gontcharova started with the conception of this as a brightly coloured work but in preparation it became progressively more stark and abstract, until the final version proved to be completely unrealistic but with a grave, almost tragic power which still seems very 'advanced' even half a century later. The next year saw an outstanding example of the other possible extreme, the Dadaist *Relâche* created by Picabia, Satie and Borlin for the Ballets Suédois.

At the same time equally original and ambitious work was being done in Russia, largely unknown at that time to people outside. There too was a conflict between those who wanted to reform the classical tradition and those who wanted a full-scale revolution against it. The latter view was that of Kasyan Goleizovsky, who became notorious with works like *Joseph the Beautiful* in 1925. In this, he and the designer Boris Erdman painted the dancers' bodies to follow a definite colour scheme. They were then made to form sculptural groups on a terraced structure, with poses passing from one to another to give the impression of living sculpture rather than dance. His choreography was acrobatic, erotic and without much dance content; this made him unpopular with the public and authorities until he later won favour as an expert on folk-dance and classicism.

Although he represented exactly the opposite approach, Fyodor Lopukhov found no more support for the most drastic of his experimental works, the *Dance Symphony*, which was given one performance only in March 1923. In this, starting with a solitary dancer walking towards the sun and shielding his eyes from the bright light of creation, and ending with all 18 dancers in a pattern supposed to represent the 'cosmogonic spiral', Lopukhov tried to suggest the whole cycle of life in the universe by abstract patterns to Beethoven's Fourth Symphony.

However muddled and obscure the imagery may have been, the work foreshadowed and established the principles of much that was to follow. It was, by the nature of its cast (friends of the choreographer who gave up their summer holiday the previous year for its creation), likely to be a very influential work. The dancers included Georgi Balanchivadze, who as Balanchine later became the most prolific and widely produced choreographer in America and Europe; Leonid Ivanov, who as Lavrovsky became one of the leading Soviet choreographers; future directors of the Bolshoi Ballet and the Leningrad Ballet School; and also the subsequently famous ballerina Alexandra Danilova.

Lopukhov's theory was that there should be 'dance symphonies
. . . free of the close limitations of the story and accessories with
which old ballets were encumbered. The art of dancing is great
for the very reason that it is capable of conveying by itself,
through the medium of choreography, a situation and surroundings
that are in reality unseen but felt. The art of dancing is capable of
making the spectator experience such phenomena as wind or
lightning far more strongly than scenic illusions of the same
things.'

Lopukhov believed that the curve of the choreographic shape
should correspond with that of the music, and that it was even
'possible to convey choreographically the change in musical
tonality' with, for instance, the major key corresponding to outward and the minor key to inward movements. 'Movements and
music are linked together by the discipline of rhythm. Dance
should flow from the movement and they should both speak of the
same things. Music that depicts soaring cannot be bound to a
choreographic theme of crawling, even if the dance and music are
identical rhythmically.' He was not content however with mere
'music visualization' but declared that 'choreographic themes
should be worked out like musical themes on the principle of
antagonism, parallel development and contrast, not on the principle of stringing together casual steps'.

Lopukhov's arguments seem to anticipate those which raged in
the west during the 1930s when Leonide Massine introduced the
so-called symphonic ballet, namely a ballet arranged to symphonic
music. Tchaikovsky, Brahms, Berlioz, Beethoven and Shostakovich in turn were called in aid over a six-year period, 1933–9,
during which the aesthetic justification and even the morality of
this kind of ballet were fiercely argued on both sides. But these
works did not really abandon narrative content; even *Choreartium*
(to Brahms's Fourth Symphony), the most abstract of them, was
conceived in terms of a fresco at Siena, a fête champêtre, renaiss-
ance noblemen and so on, and interpreted by most spectators in
literary terms too. In *La Symphonie Fantastique* the music had a
programme justifying the detailed plot, but the other works tagged
a specific 'meaning' on to a self-sufficient score, sometimes with
more success than others: *Les Présages* (to Tchaikovsky's Fifth
Symphony) could probably work even now if danced by a company
like the Bolshoi.

While these works were exciting great enthusiasm and equal
abuse, two other choreographers were working tentatively and
pragmatically towards a different way of handling symphonic
music in dance form. Frederick Ashton's *Les Rendezvous* in 1933
was set to very light music (a suite arranged from pieces by Auber)
and the choreographer disclaimed 'any serious portent', but in its
choreographic structure the work went much further than the
divertissement which might have been expected, proving to be

as much a unified whole as, say, *Les Sylphides*. It was the first step
on the path that was to lead to the masterly *Symphonic Variations*
thirteen years later, which proved and has remained the supreme
embodiment of the English classic style.

George Balanchine's *Serenade*, to Tchaikovsky's Serenade for
Strings, in 1934, evolved from classes in stage technique which the
choreographer started for his young pupils when he founded the
School of American Ballet. He later explained:

It seemed to me that the best way to make students aware of
stage technique was to give them something new to dance,
something they had never seen before . . . The class contained,
the first night, seventeen girls and no boys. The problem was,
how to arrange this odd number of girls so that they would look
interesting. I placed them on diagonal lines and decided that
the hands should move first to give the girls practice . . . The
next class contained only nine girls; the third, six. I
choreographed to the music with the pupils I happened to
have at a particular time. Boys began to attend the class and
they were worked into the pattern. One day, when all the girls
rushed off the floor area we were using as a stage, one of the
girls fell and began to cry. I told the pianist to keep on playing
and kept this bit in the dance. Another day, one of the girls
was late for class, so I left that in too . . . Many people think
there is a concealed story in the ballet. There is not.

Like Ashton, Balanchine took a long time before he carried the
almost accidentally invented new form to its logical conclusion.
This came about when he created two new works for a 'good-will
tour' of Latin America by the American Ballet in 1941. He had
seen the careful revival of Fokine's *Les Sylphides* prepared by the
choreographer the previous year for Ballet Theatre's opening
season and had been struck by its beauty. He realized that of all
Fokine's ballets, this was the most enduring, although with its
complete lack of plot it ran directly opposite to Fokine's published
theories of how a ballet should be made, theories which until then
would have had lip service at least from most people. He decided
that what Fokine had done, he too could do.

One of the two works he then created was *Concerto Barocco*, set
to Bach's Double Violin Concerto in D minor. Balanchine felt it
necessary to defend his choice of music from a possible charge that
this score can stand alone and needs no 'filling out' with dancing;
he commented that 'bad music often inspires bad dancing, bad
choreography,' and went on:

A choreographer disinterested in classical dancing will not care
to use scores by Bach and Mozart except for theatrical
sensational reasons; he will select music more to his immediate
purpose. But if the dance designer sees in the development of
classical dancing a counterpart in the development of music

and has studied them both, he will derive continual inspiration from great scores. He will also be careful, as he acts on this inspiration, not to interpret the music beyond its proper limits, not to stretch the music to accommodate a literary idea, for instance. If the score is a truly great one, suitable for dancing, he will not have need of such devices and can present his impression in terms of pure dance.

Concerto Barocco was an exercise in pure baroque classicism. The other plotless ballet Balanchine made at the same time, *Ballet Imperial* (to Tchaikovsky's Piano Concerto No. 2), was meant as a tribute to Petipa, 'the father of the classic ballet', and his greatest composer. Although plotless it has hints of a courtly and ceremonious situation, and it might be thought of as an abstraction of a typical Petipa evening-long ballet: the first movement corresponding to the introduction of the characters and exposition of their relationships, the second to the more or less obligatory romantic 'vision scene' and the third to the festive celebrations which normally concluded the long ballets of the late nineteenth century.

The success of these works led to many more, but Balanchine was always tactful enough to avoid the grand masterpieces of the symphonic repertory. The symphonies he used were by Bizet, Gounod, Mendelssohn or Tchaikovsky (Third Symphony), more often he turned to concerti, divertimenti, suites or short orchestral works. Not that these were always, or even often, unadventurous; he and Martha Graham between them in *Episodes* set dances to the complete orchestral works of Webern. By that time, however, he had already begun to develop a new technique for such music.

This began with *The Four Temperaments*, described as 'a dance ballet without plot' to a commissioned score by Hindemith, in which composer and choreographer both took as their starting point the ancient idea of the human organism being made up of four different temperaments or humours. Sanguinic and choleric could be easily enough expressed in straightforward classic dancing, but for melancholic and phlegmatic it was necessary to invent movement that was rather different: it inclined to turn in rather than out, to sink instead of aspiring as classic choreography generally does.

The movements were developed a lot further when Balanchine later made a ballet to Schoenberg's Opus 34, the first time he had tackled a twelve-tone composition. As the music is short, and in order to familiarize audiences with its unfamiliar qualities, it was played twice. Balanchine explained that 'the first time, I hoped, would focus people's eyes enough for them to hear the music better and the second time it was played maybe they would understand. The first part of the ballet therefore had no story. It was about the music and attempted to look like it sounded, as new and odd, if you like, as people once found Schoenberg's idea that you should make music with twelve notes rather than the usual seven notes of the scale.' Then on the repeat of the music came an attempt to interpret the ideas of threat, danger, fear and catas-trophe which occur in the composer's titles for the music's sections. It was the first, plotless part which provided the seed of other works by Balanchine to twelve-tone music, including Stravin-sky's *Agon* and his share of *Episodes*. Movement becomes intricate and angular, hips and feet jut out at unusual angles, the weight of the body is often oddly carried, partnering is strenuous rather than elegant. The music led to a new choreographic vocabulary, while simultaneously Balanchine continued his former open, frank style when working to more conventional scores.

MARTHA GRAHAM AND HER CONTEMPORARIES

Because she has endured such an extraordinary time in the theatre, far more than the dancer's normal span, Martha Graham is both a predecessor and a contemporary of the next generation, even the next two generations of modern dancers. You have only to look at some of her roles (the Mary figure in *El Penitente*, say, or the wife in *Appalachian Spring*) to see how prettily she must once have danced; but with time her roles became more static, a brooding figure looking back into memories that are acted out by the others around her. The apotheosis of this approach is her only full-evening work, *Clytemnestra*, in which the incidents of the Greek tragedy are picked out fitfully as if by flashes of lightning in the darkness of a haunted mind, while she sits or stalks in regal but solitary gloom.

This is the image which Graham primarily presents nowadays, and it is a misleading one because it reveals only half of her achievement. There were the lyrical dances too; formerly for herself, latterly to show off the young dancers of her company; there was the Americana, of which *Appalachian Spring* is only the most famous example; and there was—luckily there remained, wickedly glinting even in her final years—the comic sense too.

A curious thing about her comic ballets however is that they reveal how deep-seated in her imagination was some of the imagery that occurs in the darker works. In *Every Soul is a Circus*, a woman's mind is seen as a circus ring complete with whip-cracking ringmaster. In *Acrobats of God* the dancer's daily barre becomes a kind of altar, and the man with the whip appears again, this time as the balletmaster who dominates dancers and choreographer alike. *Part Real, Part Dream* contrasts a harsh aggressiveness with a gentle sensitivity; the dominating character steps from a structure that is like a combination of a pissoir and a fortress.

Aggression is never far from the surface in Graham's ballets, nor cruelty, both with heavy sexual overtones. Male characters

C

tend to carry outsized weapons, the symbolic sense of which is fairly obvious; even St Michael in *Seraphic Dialogue* subdues the warrior Joan with his great sword before her martyrdom. In the serious works, every bed is also like a grave, and the heroines (Clytemnestra, Jocasta, Judith, Medea, Phaedra) are often women who destroyed men. Miss Graham is an upright respectable American lady of Puritan stock, but her ballets seethe with emotion which, had it been expressed in words rather than action, would have had difficulty getting itself performed on public stages until recently.

This is part of the explanation of her immense influence: she opened up untouched areas of the mind to theatrical expression. Now that creative taste has swung another way, to a cooler approach, it is easy to suggest that some of Graham's ballets are morbid, but they won new possibilities of expressiveness for dancing, and they make a powerful theatrical impact. When Holofernes' head rolls gruesomely across the stage in a sheet, apparently bereft of its owner, or Orestes hurls his axe after the fleeing Aegisthus, or Oedipus falls like an overthrown statue from his plinth to the floor, the combination of surprise and inevitability in the action is overwhelming, and the physical image sums up character and occasion in an unforgettable way.

Like Tudor in classical ballet, Graham explored the possibility of psychological expression in movement of human nature under stress, and like Tudor she has had no direct successor in this, but has enriched the possibilities of insight into characterization in one direction, possibilities used obliquely by others where she worked directly.

Besides, as I said, these intense dark works of hers are only part of her range, created round the unusual gifts of herself and her leading dancers at a particular stage of her career. Without them, I suspect the works would not make the same effect and are unlikely to survive. Other dances of hers are more likely to continue being performed, such as the luminous *Seraphic Dialogue*, in which four aspects of Joan of Arc (maid, warrior, martyr and saint) are shown and reconciled; or *Embattled Garden*, in which Adam and Eve, Lilith and the Serpent dance a witty rondo of temptation and fall. Or the lyrical-dramatic *Errand into the Maze*, with its heroine daunted by her own sexual fears (represented by a man wearing horns on his head and a yoke which binds his arms into the shape of a crucifix) who eventually comes to terms with this minotaur and brings light and straightness to the labyrinth of her own mind.

Each of these works just mentioned exemplifies another aspect of Graham's style which has had widespread influence, namely the use of a setting designed by a sculptor—usually, as in all these instances, Isamu Noguchi. For St Joan, a few shapes in fine golden wire suggest the gates of heaven. A board with holes cut in it, set about by a few upright rods, and overlooked by a 'tree'

consisting of a slender upright post with two horizontal projections, sufficiently places the garden of Eden. For the labyrinth,
two slim posts and an entwined thread are all that is needed.
What these shapes and structures have in common is that they
are brought into the action and vitally affect in some way the
manner of movement.

In *Embattled Garden* for instance the Serpent hangs upside down
from the tree, and everyone dances in and through the holes,
platform and swaying rods of the other structure. In *Errand* the
rope represents the maze, defining the path of movement, and its
unravelling provides the key to the final resolution. In *Seraphic
Dialogue*, Joan's angels slide in and out of heaven under or round the
gates, and she is at last lifted up to be enthroned among them.

This last work was in fact developed from a solo which Graham
had previously danced (*The Triumph of St Joan*). When she
expanded it into dramatic form with different dancers playing the
different aspects of Joan, the choreographer told the designer what
she felt about the character but did not stipulate any special
requirements for the setting. When she saw the result her comment
was 'That's it, now we have to learn to use it.' She explains that
'a set for me is nothing unless it is used. I'm not interested in a
backdrop. I don't want a static. I'm not saying that it can't be
wonderful, but I've never wanted to do it and I've never tried.'
So each of her works takes place in its own distinctive setting
(only very rarely nowadays does she use a completely bare stage)
which contributes to the total effect far more than was customary
in older dance works. In the dance theatre, Graham has always put
as much stress on theatre as on dance.

The older generation of American modern dancers presented
works which were either straightforward dances or had a firm
narrative structure. Among Graham's contemporaries, Doris
Humphrey was notable for the subtle musicality and unhackneyed
use of space right from her early *New Dance* onwards. Even then,
in the early 1930s, she had, as she later wrote, 'discarded the idea of
music visualization. It seemed quite unnecessary, and indeed false,
to force the dance to follow music exactly. The two arts have such
utterly different media that the dance could only be damaged by
being cut to fit every phrase, every beat and every measure. More-
over it was a redundant practice. As the composer has said it all
once, why repeat it in movement terms? So I evolved a theory of
relating the dance to the music, while leaving each its individuality
intact. This results in a dance and music partnership, in which
neither dominates or imitates the other, in short a true collaboration.'

A similar relationship was developed when she used the words
of a poem by Garcia Lorca in *Lament for Ignacio Sanchez Mejias*,
about the famous bullfighter, in one of the works she created for

her most illustrious pupil, José Limón. 'I see words as a means of conveying facts,' she wrote, 'and the dance as the means of expressing emotion.' Limón himself, an immensely impressive dancer, was also a choreographer, less delicately subtle perhaps than Humphrey but more powerfully theatrical. He tended, without abandoning the literary basis of his dances, to distil them into a condensed form; in this way he converted the story of Othello into an almost formal suite of dances, *The Moor's Pavane*, where the violence when it bursts out is the more overwhelming by contrast with the preceding artificiality. Even in a work like *There is a Time*, where the interest is primarily in the contrast of different dance moods, the structure of the work is dictated by a theme from Ecclesiastes that 'To everything there is a season, and a time to every purpose under the heavens', giving rise to variations on the idea of a time for mourning, laughing, silence, clamour, sowing and reaping, living and dying, framed in a round dance for all the participants. It is a mark, incidentally, of the way ballet and modern dance were growing together that during 1970 both these works were revived by Limón for classical ballet companies, American Ballet Theatre and the Royal Swedish Ballet.

Cut off from the mainstream of American dance in his studio in Los Angeles, Lester Horton was pursuing remarkably similar lines to those East Coast artists who were in a position to influence each other. Starting with spectacles of American Indian dances, he went on to develop his own theatrical style of dance, most typically represented perhaps (since he did six different versions of it over a period of 16 years) by a choreodrama *Salome*. The most widely known of his works are two short duets revived by the Alvin Ailey company after Horton's death: a grim drama of puritan intolerance, *The Beloved*, and *To José Clemente Orozco* based on the revolutionary murals of the Mexican painter. The fact that he adopted independently so many ideas also tried out elsewhere (constructed sets, for instance, and the introduction of speech, as well as themes in some instances dealing with politically topical subjects) suggests that these developments were meeting an inevitable need of their time.

Equally inevitably, there was later a reaction against the older attitudes, although these continued in a few instances. Anna Sokolow's gloomy but sometimes gripping dance works occupy a kind of middle ground. In *Rooms* (about people who 'meet each other, pass each other, but there's no communication—that's New York, you live next to somebody and you never speak to them') the episodes reveal individual characters. In *Opus '65* there is non-specific but detailed structure like that which Robbins had adopted some years earlier. In *Deserts*, in which she abandoned her usual jazz accompaniment for a mixed orchestral and electronic score by Varèse, the intimations of emptiness and loneliness become abstract and organized into a more symphonic form.

MAN OF ALL WORLDS—JEROME ROBBINS

Jerome Robbins sprang into prominence suddenly one night in April 1944 as the first major American ballet choreographer. Other Americans before him had made some interesting ballets but these paled into insignificance compared either with what an emigré choreographer like Balanchine was achieving in the classic ballet or other Americans were doing in modern dance forms. Robbins's *Fancy Free* was in form a pure classic ballet with a show-off demi-caractère technique including some importations from the dance halls and some vaudeville tricks; but what the audience noticed was not the technique, it was the characterization, the comedy, the contemporary setting ('Time: the present' declared the programme) and the sheer theatrical punch of an idea that was soon to be reworked by its choreographer and composer, Leonard Bernstein, into an equally successful musical, *On the Town*.

We ought to bear in mind that in the context of ballet at that time (or even now), a work which put recognizable contemporary types on stage with the vividness of *Fancy Free* was in a sense very experimental, almost revolutionary. Primarily, however, the early Robbins was a sheer entertainer until he turned to the theme of three insecure people and their relationships in *Facsimile*. Later he both expanded and developed a theme similar to this in his *Age of Anxiety* (based on Auden's long poem) and also came under the influence of Balanchine to the extent of treating a theme which might have been that of race relationships, or alternatively a Montagues and Capulets situation, in almost completely abstract terms in *The Guests*. His best works continued to explore human character in terms closely related to pure dance. One such was *Afternoon of a Faun* in which he used the same Debussy music as Nijinsky employed for his first ballet and created a real-life modern situation analogous to the mythological theme Nijinsky used. The faun and nymph became in this version two dancers in a studio, so narcissistically concerned about themselves and their work that a gentle kiss on the cheek seemed like a violation and caused the girl to go off in a mood of startled amazement.

Simultaneously with his ballet career Robbins became an exceptionally successful choreographer and director of stage and film musicals, being responsible for the whole conception of *West Side Story* and for the dances in *Fiddler on the Roof* among many others. He also directed plays and spent some time working on a project for an American Lyric Theatre Workshop which was to combine stage, musical and dance elements in a new way and reflect contemporary American culture. Although the workshop project has so far been abortive, its aims have been present in much of Robbins's work.

Between 1958 and 1962 Robbins presented (mainly in Europe) occasional seasons by a company of his own formation, Ballets:

USA. For this his most popular production was *N Y Export: Opus Jazz* which used a mixture of jazz and other dance techniques in a semi-abstract suite with strong emotional overtones. *Events* carried this process further, although with less success. Even in these strongly jazz-influenced works Robbins kept a cool style that owed something to his classical background but even more to American attitudes and manners.

As his own master, running his own company, Robbins could afford to do what he liked. Both *N Y Export* and *Events* showed a serious awareness of and concern for major political and social problems. The former, although ostensibly just a dance suite, contained intimations of violence in the section called 'Statics' and of loneliness in the 'Passage for two'. *Events* dealt with various themes including a homosexual relationship with one partner looking for love, the other only for sex; a Negro entertainer or sportsman lionized and then thrown over by white society; people clamouring for a god who fails them; and finally the H-bomb and its effects.

Robbins at this time said that 'right now, in the way I'm working . . . a theme of pure dance attracts me' but went on to add that 'I don't think any ballet says nothing. Because first of all it's being performed by humans, which immediately communicates something. But I use the word "abstract" not meaning "non-representational" but in the sense that I have abstracted from any subject the core, the essence of the feeling, the atmosphere. There are no specifics, let's say the jazz ballet that we do is abstract in contrast to the specifics of *West Side Story*. However, it happens to deal with teen-age problems . . . There are no characters, there are no situations. There is mood, there is atmosphere, there is a strong emotion.'

All this was dealt with in a very cool way; as Robbins explained: ' "Play it cool" is what we say . . . a lot may be going on underneath, a lot of emotion, a lot of passion, perhaps even a lot of sexuality, but don't, don't show it.' Although this attitude later became widely emulated, it was at the time a specifically American approach.

Robbins then was interested in the idea that 'the dance communicates to the audience in a way that no other theatre art can'. He wanted themes that 'cannot be done better as a play or as an opera or as a piece of music or as a painting or any of the other arts'. His aim was 'that the emotion in the audience is aroused and evoked . . . through things that cannot be said, and that movement to movement makes the emotion rather than the specifics or a silent movie technique'.

He was also keen however on the idea that 'a theatre performer, whether they're in opera, play or ballet company, should be able to do and perform all the theatre arts—I think it's a terrible thing to have a singer come on stage and just use their voice and a dancer just to come on stage and use their body. I think they're on the stage for a dramatic purpose . . . and they should be able to project that.' He felt that 'there is a trend in America to fuse all the theatre arts' and that the dancers were leading this trend because they 'are a little more daring, and a little freer and a little more aggressive in their desire to extend themselves'. A great deal of Robbins's time over the next few years was taken up with different ways of trying to bring about this fusion of the arts, but when he finally returned to ballet it was with a work which took up many of his earlier approaches but treated them in a more classical (although also more personal) way than before.

This was *Dances at a Gathering*, created in 1969 for New York City Ballet and mounted the following year for the Royal Ballet. The music is by Chopin (not orchestrated but played on the piano), the duration more than an hour. Robbins said, 'I didn't know it was going to be that long a ballet or what it was going to be . . . it's almost like an artist who has not been drawing for a long time. I didn't know how my hand would be. And I was so surprised that the dances began to come out.' Starting with the idea of making just a pas de deux, he began to think in terms of a pas de six, worked in rehearsal with whoever was available and ended up with a cast of ten. The sequence of dances is light and casual, like friends dancing together on some special occasion; classical and character dances combine in a smooth flow; the dancers do not play roles but just convey the sense of their own characters. Outwardly it is a very traditional ballet, yet in feeling it has a freshness and originality greater than most works more consciously experimental in purpose. Perhaps the moral is that the attitudes of a lifetime count for much more than the intentions of the moment.

A CHANCE FOR DANCE—JOHN CAGE AND MERCE CUNNINGHAM

Every artist walks a tightrope between intention and achievement. With Merce Cunningham, the problem of proceeding from one to the other is complicated by the likelihood that at any moment he will abandon that look of solemn concentration in favour of an impish grin, and decide to turn cartwheels or walk on his hands. Sometimes in consequence he comes a cropper, but when he does stay up the result is infinitely more spectacular and entertaining than would otherwise be the case. In less metaphorical terms, Cunningham is unpredictable, variable, not in the least bound by what he thinks he ought to be; occasionally silly but never pompous and never, never to be taken for granted. His greatest capacity is his power to take nothing on trust; his greatest blessing, a gift of anarchical humour; his greatest talent, for dancing that is unexpected as well as delightful.

I stress straight away Cunningham's sheer skill as a dancer and his gift of comedy, because in writing about his work it is easy to make him sound rather frightening, which he is not. Even at his most avant-garde (and nobody is ahead of him in the field),

Cunningham is always entertaining. In fact he began as a straight-forward entertainer. In his home town of Centralia, Washington, he learned tap, folk and exhibition ballroom dancing; and he had briefly toured the vaudeville and nightclub circuit in Oregon and California before Martha Graham invited him to join her company as a soloist in 1940.

The roles she created for him included the vaultingly dominating Christ figure in *El Penitente*; lithe, springy March in *Letter to the World*; and the ecstatic Revivalist in *Appalachian Spring*. All these revealed aspects of his remarkable dance personality, but his subsequent career has also shown strong influences both of his early activities in vaudeville and of the classical ballet he studied while dancing with Graham: the latter influence far less in technique than in the line and shape of his work.

The other important influences on Cunningham have been his collaboration with the composer John Cage and with various contemporary American painters. Cage in particular, an associate since the earliest days of Cunningham's own independent choreography, has been a constant spur to new audacities. Separately, Cage and Cunningham would each have made a mark on contemporary music, theatre and dance; together, the effect of their work has been not so much doubled as squared.

This pair can, at times, be puzzling, especially to the person with a background of dance activity but perhaps less awareness of the way things are developing in the other arts. Take, for instance, *Variations V*. The music was a development of a concert Cage had given at the Feigen–Palmer Gallery, Los Angeles, mixing sounds picked up by microphones above the bar, in the gallery and at the street door, together with other pre-recorded elements of music or speech. In *Variations V*, the 'electronic gadgetry' (Cage's own expression) was actuated by the movements of the dancers. The sound-sources, Cunningham explains, were two-fold: 'The first was a series of poles, 12 in all, like antennae, placed over the stage, each to have a sound radius, sphere-shaped, of 4 feet. When a dancer came into this radius a sound would result. The second sound-source was a series of photo-electric cells, figured out by Billy Klüver of the Bell Laboratories, which were to sit on the floor along the sides of the stage. The stage lights would be focused in such a way as to hit them, and when a dancer passed between a sound could happen. This didn't work out exactly as the stage lights were too distant to strike strongly enough to the sides of the stage. So at the last minute the cells were put at the base of the 12 poles throughout the area and this seemed to function. The general principle as far as I was concerned was like the doors opening when you go into the supermarket.' The kind of sound, its duration or repetition, was controlled by musicians with various machines including tape recorders, oscillators and shortwave radios.

Just to make matters more complicated, two films were shown simultaneously on the backcloth; these included rehearsal sequences by Cunningham and the dancers, and giant close-ups of Cunningham's feet. In addition, various coloured slides were projected apparently at random, sometimes right way up, sometimes not; while at the same time the dancers solemnly went through their allotted movements and if you looked hard enough, without being distracted by the other elements, you could see that there was some fine dancing hidden away there.

As if this was not enough, some extra novelties were introduced. Cunningham and later Carolyn Brown potted and repotted a large plant at one side of the stage; this had a cartridge microphone attached which could produce sound at any quiver. Barbara Lloyd, wearing on her head a towel with a contact microphone attached, stood on her head and was rocked back and forth. Cunningham at one point bounced on a mattress wired for sound, and at the end of the work rode a bicycle round the stage, passing all the poles and electric cells, then quietly off.

Considered as an ordinary ballet, *Variations V* was hopeless; but as an unusual experience it was extraordinarily stimulating. An interviewer in *Ballet Review*, referring to Marshall McLuhan's famous phrase, asked Cunningham 'Was this the extensions of man?' and was given the answer 'It was more an extension of the theatre in the directions that the society is being expanded, that is, technology (and at breakneck speed, too).'

Often Cunningham's works pose similar problems of taking in many different stimuli at once. In *How to Pass, Kick, Fall and Run* the dancers made wonderfully free, smooth, open, sporty movements, sometimes playing each other at imaginary games, sometimes in teams, sometimes determinedly alone. Cunningham himself seemed to be the archetypal champion: solitary, pleased and condescending.

While this was happening, a man (John Cage or sometimes David Vaughan) sat at the side of the stage with a table, book, stopwatch and microphone, reading out anecdotes by Cage, mostly about his life or sometimes Cunningham's. These stories varied from night to night; the only requirement of the 'score' was that they should be read one per minute, regardless of length. Most were amusing, but of course they had no connexion with what the dancers were doing, so you had two different things, the dancing and the story, competing for attention, which some people found confusing. Yet most people can manage, when it suits them, to read a newspaper and conduct a conversation simultaneously; or cope at once with food and television; so why not two separate but concurrent activities in the theatre? Incidentally, Cunningham's own explanation of the work is simple: 'I am a practical man (the theatre demands it). We had to have one simple dance in terms of sets and costumes, setting up and rehearsing—and the sound.'

It was Cage who probably influenced Cunningham to introduce chance elements into choreography as he himself was doing into music. This factor in Cunningham's work is often over-emphasized and misunderstood: many of his dances, once created, are absolutely set. Chance, indeed, can be used in the creation of a work which is then immutable. Cunningham used this method to create three solos for himself, dividing the body into parts, listing the possibilities of those parts and then tossing coins to select movements. Unfortunately, as Carolyn Brown has recorded: 'he discovered that the execution of the resulting movement was nearly impossible, and it took months of rehearsal to accomplish it. In *Lavish Escapade*, some of the final movement superimpositions were so difficult he was never able to realize them completely. Clearly this was not a practical method for making group works.'

Since 1951, very few of Cunningham's works have been made without some use of chance procedures, but what, how and how much has varied. Having been involved in many of them as one of Cunningham's leading dancers, Carolyn Brown wrote that 'The particular procedures used varied considerably with each dance. It is possible to arrive at the time structure, the movements, the form, the continuity, the space, the number of people on stage at one time, whether dancers dance together or separately, all by chance methods.'

Cunningham's first attempt was in fact very simple. Having decided to base a long work (*Sixteen dances for soloist and company of three*) on the nine permanent emotions of the Indian classical theatre, 'four light and four dark with tranquillity the ninth and pervading one,' he 'could find no reason why a specific light should follow a specific dark and thereupon threw a coin'.

But it was not by any means always so easy. For *Suite by Chance* (1953) he took several hours daily for several months to prepare elaborate charts of possible durations, movements, extensions, including also elements of silence or stasis, and then threw coins to pick combinations of these. Cunningham's motive was not unlike that which sent Alwin Nikolais exploring a rather different direction: 'It was almost impossible to see a movement in the modern dance during that period not stiffened by literary or personal connection, and the simple, direct and unconnected look of this dance (which some thought abstract and dehumanized) disturbed.' To bring out these qualities, the movements in his working charts were purposely 'as unadorned and flat as I could make them.' His own reaction in working on the piece was how strongly it let the personality of each dancer appear.

From using chance in composing what then becomes a set work, it is a small but fearsome leap to the use of chance in performance, allowing the final work to be indeterminate. Cunningham adopted this in works such as *Field Dances*, which is designed to be done anywhere. The number of dancers and the total length of performance may vary. Each dancer is given one, two or three short dances 'he can deal with as he chooses' and there are certain things they can do together. Each dancer may leave or enter the stage when he wishes, may adopt his own speed, may repeat or omit from his own allotted movements.

The likelihood of two performances of *Field Dances* being identical is remote, to say the least; so can it really be regarded as a work with a continuing identity from one performance to another, or is each performance really a new work? Having seen several performances of it on different occasions, I think the answer is clearly that, however much it changes, *Field Dances* retains an identity which enables you to recognize it from one occasion to another.

The same is true of *Story*, so called because there was 'no implicit or explicit narrative but . . . every spectator may see and hear the events in his own way'. Carolyn Brown contrasts this with a piece like *Rune*, which was made in five sections of five minutes each, capable of being done in any order: 'However, the technical difficulty of the dance necessitated fixing the order well in advance of each performance to insure sufficient rehearsal of the transitions from section to section.' In the case of *Story*, on the other hand:

The dancers discovered the order and time of the sections of the dance only a few minutes before the curtain went up on that dance. Indeterminate elements affected every area of this work: a different set was made by Rauschenberg on the day of each performance from objects found in the particular theater. The costumes (in addition to a basic 'ground' of leotard and tights), gathered by Rauschenberg from second-hand shops, Army–Navy stores, the Salvation Army, found on the street and in the theater etc., were selected by the dancers from the pile which grew and changed. My favorite memory is of Barbara Lloyd putting on all the costumes she could manage, leaving the rest of us with next to nothing, and making herself so large and encumbered she could barely move. What effect this had on the choreography was interesting indeed. The music by Toshiro Ichiyanagi called for rubbed sounds. The musicians used the entire theater—auditorium, backstage and on stage—as sound sources. Naturally each theater provided an enormous variety of surfaces. The choreography itself offered the dancers a certain amount of freedom: given phrases of movement, the dancers were free to vary them in the space, direction, order of continuity, speed and dynamics. At times they were free to relate to others on stage or to ignore them. In some instances, they could remain off stage if they so chose. In one section, the dancers were given direction and level, and length of time in the particular direction and level, but the movement was completely of the dancers' own devising, with just one 'rule': the dancer had to remain attached to one place in the space with at least one foot throughout the time span (which varied) except once, when the dancer was allowed to move into another area by a body's length and continue. This section was improvised, or should have been. Cunningham expected the dancers to choreograph spontaneously and not pre-set and rehearse and repeat. This proved to be more difficult for some than others.

One consequence of this (strictly predetermined) indeterminacy was that the non-existent 'story' of *Story* could change a lot from one night to another. Sometimes it was frighteningly grim, at others comic. The first time Cunningham showed it in London, on the opening of his first season there, happened to be a rather dull performance; later ones were gripping, but only those who returned, or first came to see him later in the season, could know this. Why take such a risk? One likely explanation (apart from any personal predilection) is that by letting in the element of chance, you may achieve something more exciting, more dramatic or beautiful, than would have come about without this element. Cunningham wrote of one of his solos, choreographed by chance processes, that 'the dance as performed seems to have an un-mistakable dramatic intensity in its bones. It seems to me that it was simply a question of "allowing" this quality to happen rather than of "forcing" it. It is this "tranquillity" of the actor or the dancer which seems to me essential. A "tranquillity" which allows him to detach himself and thereby *to present* freely and liberally.' Yet he also remarked 'the trouble with chance is that people think it's a gimmick—but it's no more a gimmick than the Grand Canyon is. I think I've accepted chance that way because I'm basically intuitive.'

The tranquillity Cunningham speaks of is something present in his own performances and in those of his best dancers. Cunningham himself is unusually tall and wiry in build (not a conventional dancer's shape) with a lived-in, weather-beaten face. He has an extraordinary physical command, as likely to show itself in tiny movements as in big ones, and an uncommon sense of rhythm. These qualities help to explain certain characteristics of his choreography: in particular, the way he uses both space and time. He uses the whole performing area, not just the focal centre on which many choreographers and producers rely; sometimes (*Summerspace* is an example) he will create a deliberately un-focused dance, inviting the eye to wander through the patterns instead of (as customary) seducing it to a specific key point. Space in its other sense is important to him too, namely the space between movements, also the space between events. Just as Cage lets silence form part of his music, so Cunningham lets stillness form part of his ballets.

So far as the use of music is concerned, what Cunningham noted about *Suite by Chance* appears to be true of most, maybe all of his works: 'The relationship between the dance and music is one of co-existence, that is, being related simply because they exist at the same time.' This explains how the score or the choreography can be variable without disastrous consequences. Generally they start and finish together (but not always—*Winterbranch*, for instance, is an exception) but are not otherwise directly related. This makes things harder, not easier, for the choreographer and dancer, since absolute synchronization is necessary without the chance of sustaining rhythm by the musical beat; also for the audience, who must respond simultaneously to separate stimuli.

Handled by anyone of less talent, the number and variety of new approaches which Cunningham tries would probably lead to disaster. Only because he is so skilled in his own crafts (as choreographer, dancer, artist, entertainer) can he afford to break the rules. Also, he can afford to collaborate with leading painters and musicians and not be overshadowed by them.

Cage has long been his musical director; other composers (David Tudor, Gordon Mumma) play the electric machines in the orchestra pit. Rauschenberg was previously in charge of the visual aspects of the performance; at present Jasper Johns has this function. These are all very advanced in their own fields, but when asked what it means to be 'avant-garde' Cunningham replied 'The question doesn't fit me. I've never applied it to myself, any more than I have the word abstract.' The fact remains that at his performances the audience can also see and hear the work of leading American painters, sculptors and musicians, thus attracting spectators who would not normally go to ballet, and who respond to Cunningham perhaps with an understanding a typical ballet audience would not share. When he played in Paris in 1970, only two London newspapers reviewed his performances; one sent its ballet critic, the other its art critic.

What matters finally, of course, is the finished product rather than the process. Cunningham's methods and his collaborators are important because they and Cunningham get good results. Some of his works linger in the mind long afterwards as a catalyst of the imagination. One such is *Winterbranch*. Half of it is done in silence, half to LaMonte Young's *Two Sounds*, remorselessly amplified to the threshold of pain. Leaps, falls, huddled groups, a body dragged from the stage—these are some of the elements darkly glimpsed in the intermittently lit darkness. Cunningham was asked whether there was a story to it, and quoted several interpretations that had been put to him: bombed cities; concentration camps; nuclear war; shipwreck. The last, he said, was his favourite, but 'Right you are if you think you are. I prefer directness, but that's not always possible in a society so indirect. The facts I dealt with were: people falling; light at night in our time as it strikes objects; and the formal shape of entering (walking into) an arena, a space; beginning and completing a figure, done by one or more persons; and walking out of the arena.'

He also explained on another occasion that 'the lighting is done freely each time, differently, so that the rhythms of the movements are differently accented and the shapes differently seen partially or not at all. I asked Robert Rauschenberg to think of the light as though it were night instead of day. I don't mean night as referred to in romantic pieces, but night as it is in our time with automobiles on highways, and flashlights in faces, and the eyes being deceived about shapes by the way light hits them.'

Another work in which shifting light plays a part is *Canfield*. Robert Morris's design for this consists of a vertical lighting batten hung in front of the stage, moving from side to side, regularly at first but later irregularly. This passes at intervals between the spectators and the dancers, but casts a strong pillar of light on the backcloth, thus providing the work's main illumination. The dancers are therefore at once revealed and obscured by the one object; a characteristically ingenious idea. There is also a light from above, which throws curved patterns on to the backcloth; and at the end, a portrait is projected on this cloth and all else goes dark so that the dancers are seen silhouetted against it.

The portrait is from a biography of Nicola Tesla, 'cosmic engineer', by J. J. O'Neill, and this biography inspired the score by Pauline Oliveros. This demands from the musicians an exploration on scientific lines of the acoustic qualities of the building in which they perform. Microphones are placed in different parts of the auditorium, an assistant goes off (with walkie-talkie contact maintained) to carry out specific activities in various spots, the musicians in the pit discuss the results. At a performance in Paris, conversation went like this:

Where is that sound coming from?
Down below.
Under the stage or under the hall?
The drainpipe under the stage.
Did you go down some stone steps?
Metallic.
There's a circular stone staircase.
I'll play that for you later.

In an ideal performance (so I am told by a computer musician who has actually played the piece) there would be less audible conversation and more feeling of electronic music, with the aid of tape recorders recording and playing sound samples. Even in a less than ideal interpretation, although the sounds heard would not be regarded by most people as 'music' they make a fascinating aural experience, so much so that it becomes positively difficult to watch closely what is happening on stage. This is rather a pity, but the effort is worthwhile. The dances are based on the game of patience which gives the work its title, in the sense that dances have been prepared for 13 possible deals from which a certain number are chosen for each particular performance. Sweeps of movement; stillness and activity; it would probably look marvellous on an empty stage in silence. In its theatrical context it becomes something else; whether that something is more or less than the unaccompanied dances might have been is a matter of conjecture and taste, but it is what Cunningham's nature makes it.

Yet he makes simple, uncomplex pieces too: uncomplex, that is, in the number of different simultaneous activities. For instance, the outward form of *Second Hand* is something any choreographer might have attempted: a solo, duet and group dance originally meant to be danced to music by Satie. The solo was created (under the title *Idyllic Song*) in 1945 to a two-piano arrangement by Cage of the first movement of Satie's *Socrate* for voices and orchestra. The other sections were added in 1969 but the musical copyright holders refused permission either for using Cage's arrangement or Satie's own voice and piano arrangement. So Cage, 'using *I Ching* chance operations with respect to seven modes and twelve transpositions of each, and applying these in a programmed way to his model, made a new composition preserving the rhythm' of the original; he called the result *Cheap Imitation*.

What distinguishes *Second Hand* is not anything out of the ordinary in the way of presentation, but simply the quality of the choreography: the stillness, long extensions and minute detail of hand movements in the solo for instance (danced by Cunningham), and the way in the duet he and Carolyn Brown dance separately, at a distance from each other on stage, so that the spectator's eye is forced to notice that distance and his consciousness to accept its emptiness as a vital part of the pattern, until they come suddenly and briefly together. So *Second Hand* is a good ballet to show people who, allowing their attention to be distracted, fail to notice the subtlety of Cunningham's invention in other works. The only trick of presentation is that you become aware that the tights and leotards designed by Jasper Johns start one colour on a dancer's lefthand side and fade into another on his right. Only when they all line up for their curtain calls is it apparent that they encompass the full range of the spectrum.

Johns is only one of many celebrated artists who have contributed to Cunningham's recent repertory. He even indirectly draws upon Marcel Duchamp, because an adaptation by Johns of Duchamp's *Large Glass* is part of *Walkaround Time*. Duchamp's patterns are reproduced in the form of hollow transparent plastic blocks which are set about the stage; the dancers move among these, alter their positions and finally reassemble them into a complete pattern. The choreography of *Walkaround Time* is deliberately casual; like the music (David Behrman's *for nearly an hour*) it has a break in the middle, when a radio or tape is heard uttering pop sounds and the dancers do, apparently, whatever they like, from chatting up the musicians to practising a classical ballet solo, or even disappearing off stage altogether. At the end of this break Cunningham (who acts much of the time as a lone figure set against the larger patterns) has a solo running on one spot while he completely changes his costume of sweater and tights.

Andy Warhol's silver balloons provide the décor of *RainForest*.

They are pillow-shaped, a bit more than pillow-sized, made I think of aluminized mylar and filled with helium. Some float just at stage level, others higher, even nearly up into the flies. As the dancers in their ragged costumes move among these objects, a bump or a breeze from their passing is enough to set the silver pillows bobbing gently about. One or two bounce right forward, maybe, and end in the orchestra pit; others form new obstructing patterns in the dancing area, to be set moving again by their next contact with the dancers. It is a unique and very beautiful effect.

Cunningham seems positively to welcome the designer encroaching right into the dance area or across the front of it. In *Tread*, a row of ten big industrial electric fans stand right across the proscenium arch and blow a gentle breeze into the audience. Half of them are fixed, half turn through a 180° arc, thus echoing the alternating movement and passivity which is part of the choreographic pattern.

Does some of this sound like sheer eccentricity? In practice it does not give that effect. What is so stimulating about Cunningham is that he constantly extends the dance to match new developments in the other arts and in life today. Not only that, but he has the wit, skill and intuition to make it work. Without his own achievement and his example, the dance world today would be a lot less lively.

LANDSCAPE WITH FIGURES—THE ENGLISH SCHOOL

One reason why both Ashton and Balanchine took a long time to reach the logical conclusions of their first moves towards a pure-dance classical form is that they were busy with what is in a way one of the most experimental of all dance activities: making a tradition grow where none was before. In establishing English and American ballet, they took the old Russian style on which their companies were modelled, and transformed it gradually but firmly into something different and indigenous. To see the same work danced by dancers from different lands (and this applies to old classic ballets like Petipa's or new ones like those of Ashton and Balanchine, also to the modern-dance styles of Graham or Limón, or the new-wave works of Tetley) is to appreciate the reality of national style: brought about partly by inherited characteristics and attitudes, partly by company policies, partly by training and partly by the deliberate choice of choreographers, each nation has its own way of doing the same things. Consequently, although each of the contributing artists may have markedly different qualities, it is realistic to think in terms of a British (or American, or French, Russian, etc.) school of choreography. Certainly the young British choreographers all owe a lot to Ashton, and most of them to Tudor too.

In a way Ninette de Valois, who founded the Royal Ballet, was more revolutionary than either of these. She staged in 1931 a

ballet *Job* which, inspired by William Blake's drawings, anticipated the simple, austere but expressive modern-dance style that
was to become widely accepted in Britain only after more than a
generation had passed. Her choreographic invention was never the
equal of her intelligence, however, and the only other work of hers
likely to survive is another which in a sense retrospectively brought
painters into ballet, being based on Hogarth's series *The Rake's
Progress*.

It was Antony Tudor who achieved the most profound works of
British ballet's early years. His work to Holst's orchestral suite
The Planets was an early success in the form of symphonic ballet,
with only one movement, the lyrical 'Venus', at all like traditional
ballet-making. 'Mars' was fierce and convulsive, 'Neptune' slow
and strange in its mysticism. In *Jardin aux Lilas* he showed people
in recognizable clothes, not ballet costumes, suffering recognizable
human emotions (although in what now seems the somewhat
artificial situation of an arranged marriage). *Dark Elegies* took
these emotions, deepened them and put them into the context of
an abstract expression of grief arising from some great natural
calamity causing the death of all the children in a community.
Tudor could also be wickedly and bawdily funny, but the excited
fervour he evoked among his dancers and audience was because of
the seriousness he had shown ballet to be capable of.

Then in *Pillar of Fire* Tudor invented what has been often
imitated but never equalled: the psychological ballet, showing in
outward form the inward thoughts of its heroine. It starts with an
illusion of realism: the quiet street at evening, the girl sitting on
the step, the neighbours and passers-by. Only gradually it becomes
apparent that every incident is being seen through the distorted
view of the young woman, until her jealousy, envy and desire lead
her to a madness from which after much difficulty she is led by the
continuing love of the man she first refuses to trust. Tudor himself
could not fully repeat the success of the new approach he had invented when he tried to show the making of a sex-murderer in
Undertow, but later he did manage the probably harder aim of
suggesting the growth and maturing of an innocent boy into a man
in *Shadowplay*, although on this occasion in a more symbolic and
less realistic manner.

Frederick Ashton had no such revolutionary works to offer; even
when he succeeded (in *Symphonic Variations*, *Valses Nobles et
Sentimentales* and *Scènes de Ballet*) in establishing a distinctively
British style of classical dancing the works took a long time to
win universal acceptance. He has said of *Symphonic Variations*
that he did it because while on war service and

watching the company from the outside . . . I saw that
everything was becoming much too literary, with Robert
Helpmann doing big ballets about big subjects. I thought they
were losing the dancing element and this worried me. And I

D

began thinking in terms of pure dance. Then, too, all through the war I was feeling miserable and frustrated. I didn't think I was contributing much in any direction. I got very interested in mysticism. The music of César Franck attracted me because he was also very mystical . . . I started with a very elaborate programme, nuns taking the veil and all kinds of things like that. Then I pared it all down until one day it came to me that I should use only these six dancers. But at the back of my mind there's some idea about the three girls when it starts—they're like women waiting to be fructified, so to speak—and then the man comes in. It also has elements of spring, summer and autumn, to me. There were these programmatic ideas in my own mind that I didn't necessarily want the public to know about, but that give it an emotional impact, I think, that it might not have had otherwise.

Valses Nobles et Sentimentales, on the other hand, contains hints of relationships among its performers and was, Ashton said, suggested by actual people and events; whereas *Scènes de Ballet* 'I did . . . as just an exercise in pure dancing'.

Even Ashton's traditional big-scale story ballets retained this emphasis on dancing both for decoration and, wherever possible, actually to convey the plot, and most of the younger generation of British choreographers tried to develop this line. In some ways they were in a position to go much further than he, without his prime responsibility for the basic repertory of a large, traditional state-supported company; yet he kept quietly well up with the front runners—using psychedelic lighting effects when they were still a novelty, for the setting of his *Sinfonietta*; introducing pop-art designs and a composed jazz score in *Jazz Calendar*; and most important perhaps, devising a new, cool, very modern but very classical style of dancing for his *Monotones*.

Apart from Norman Morrice, who deliberately moved with Ballet Rambert into a different style influenced by modern dance, three choreographers stand out from the next generation. Kenneth MacMillan has the most striking choreographic invention. In his dramatic works he aimed to show the spectators 'things in the ballet which they've felt in their lives . . . I want people to go to the theatre to be moved by something they can recognize.' He attempted this crudely in *The Invitation*, with realistic characters but a melodramatic plot, and more subtly in *Symphony*, where the Shostakovich music inspired a plotless work with strong threads of emotion running through it. These two parallel lines of development continue in his later work. On the one hand are pieces like *Anastasia* (based on the woman claiming to be the only survivor of the last Tsar's family) and *Checkpoint* (inspired by Orwell's novel *1984*). Both these use film projections, theatrical tricks and some small elements of electronic sound; both are concerned primarily with a rather sensational plot. In *Song of the Earth* he worked exactly the opposite way, developing from Mahler's music an abstract treatment of life and death.

MacMillan says that he has 'moved with more and more certainty towards a belief in the importance of classicism. Of course I don't mean the language of the nineteenth-century classroom, the exact steps you find in the old ballets. What I mean is the idea of a formal structure such as they used.' He works closely with the music and 'I don't think I could write dances quite independent of the music.' He does not believe in combining classical and modern dance styles: 'There's a big practical difficulty—the different kind of training needed for the two types of movement. It might perhaps be possible for men, with their greater strength. But even with them the tremendous accent which modern-style dance puts on the plié would tend to develop their legs in a way which might look odd in classical ballet.' He would like to think ballet was moving towards some kind of total theatre, 'though I'm not sure it actually is. I wouldn't hesitate myself to put in any ingredient which seemed appropriate, and certainly some modern theatre productions, like those of Peter Brook for example, seem to be moving towards a form which is pretty near to ballet.'

John Cranko also holds to the classical technique, and among his large output are many works which use it for straightforward entertainment in a traditional way, either in plotless form or in long narrative ballets. This has to some extent obscured the many innovations he has made, both of content and form. He introduced a structure in *Harlequin in April* which was far too specific to be called abstract, but far removed also from a realistic narrative, corresponding rather to lyric poetry with images of life, death, rebirth, love and enmity. Cranko believes 'that ballet should not be symbolic; it should not have an intended symbolism'. He prefers 'a relationship, a play in movement between two people on the stage. This relationship may be likened to a diamond, which has no colour in itself, but reflects varyingly, always in a different tone, for each member of the audience. It is more an "image" and each sees the image with his own eyes. We can say there is no general meaning, but each of us discovers his own metaphor.' He illustrates his point by pointing out the images in a film like *Bonnie and Clyde*, by comparison with Picasso's *Guernica*, or even the acting of Marilyn Monroe. This eclecticism is reflected in his work, which ranges from a gentle surrealism (as in his *Oiseaux Exotiques* and also some comic pieces he made for a season presented with the aid of the painter John Piper) to a frightening but non-specific dramatic situation in *The Interrogation*, which was inspired by Francis Bacon's paintings. The revue *Cranks* put movement to unexpected and often comic uses, and in the first staging of Michael Tippet's opera *The Midsummer Marriage* (which depended very much on 'images' such as Cranko admires in any art) Cranko's dances achieved a possibly unprecedented fusion of the musical and choreographic idea in an opera-ballet. In

Présence he achieved the staging envisaged by the composer Zimmermann in a new relationship of music, dance and mime gesture.

Both MacMillan and Cranko have worked with large, established companies, at Covent Garden and in Germany. Their contemporary Peter Darrell has worked principally with a small company which he helped found as Western Theatre Ballet (later, after a change of base, it became Scottish Theatre Ballet). It was meant to be 'a classical company dealing with contemporary themes' and for a long time suffered double criticism, from ballet fans who thought the themes sensational and from those who accepted the themes but thought they demanded a different technique.

Darrell's motive was the thought that 'ballet in England came to the fore partly because of the escapist value it had. It began to go its own way without particularly referring to its sister arts—the theatre, films, painting . . . There was a need to break out of this narrowness and to establish a dance-theatre company conscious of the thematic side of ballet, of content as well as form.'

His works included *The Prisoners*, about a prison escape and the subsequent jealousy and murder arising from the relationship between the two escaped men and the wife of one; *The Wedding Present* about a marriage broken up when the bride discovered her husband's former homosexual affair; *Sun into Darkness* based on a ritual murder following an orgiastic carnival in a remote Cornish village. These led to criticism of sensationalism, but Darrell defended his choice of 'basic sexual themes . . . You could do plays or films about these subjects and nobody would have called you sensational. They reflect preoccupations people have.' He objected to 'this image that classical ballet can't deal with certain subjects. It's all very well if you're in bare feet, but put on a pair of point shoes and you can't do it. It's a disservice to the art to think that. Of all the dance techniques there are, the classical technique has the widest range by far.'

In order to strengthen the theatrical effectiveness of the company's work, Darrell invited playwrights to join in the creation of new works, on the grounds that 'they know about the development of character, form and climaxes'. With John Mortimer's *Home* the idea did not work well; partly perhaps because the shape of the work did not fit the Bartók music chosen. With David Rudkin's *Sun into Darkness* the result was a logical development all through, with tightly plotted action and characters not only vivid but clearly related to each other and the action. With this work Darrell also introduced a theatrical producer, Colin Graham, to collaborate in staging it, because 'after working on a ballet for some time, one loses its theatrical perspectives'. Later, Graham helped revise other works in the repertory, 'pointing and developing characterization'.

For subject matter, Darrell likes 'people who are trapped in an environment or an inevitable situation . . . I like to see people explode'. This was the context also of his experimental creations jointly with the dramatist John Hopkins for BBC television, especially *Houseparty* in which they almost entirely eliminated recognizable dance movements, although 'it could never have been done by anyone but dancers. Each movement was timed to the beat. Even the camera work became part of the choreography.' Darrell thinks that for the small screen everything 'has to be much more concentrated and pertinent' but the stripping away of extraneous movement from *Houseparty* was in accordance with his usual style, which he defines as 'a consciousness of movement as thought . . . a complete and utter questioning of the movement one uses and of its depth and clarity in regard to the subject matter'.

THEATRE OF MAGIC—ALWIN NIKOLAIS

Alwin Nikolais always gets so much attention paid to the magical look of his creations that it is salutory to remember that one of his prime considerations is content. He began to dance during the 1930s, having been impressed by one of Mary Wigman's performances. He was at that time a musician (playing first as an accompanist for silent films, then, with the advent of talkies, for dancing classes and roadside inns), and what particularly caught his interest was Wigman's use of percussion. He went to one of her former students to learn percussion and was persuaded that for proper understanding he must study dance too. At that time, he has said, 'we were concerned very much with psychological dance and the form of dance drama such as is so beautifully done by Graham. Somehow after the war the whole idea palled with the younger dancers, and I suppose we struck out for new areas and new concerns. Our great concern was, would we have a world to practise in if we didn't know a little more about the universe? So off we went into space and the wild blue yonder, and left the other to the boudoir.'

Hence the fact that in *Imago* (subtitled 'The City Curious') Nikolais is depicting an entire imaginary civilization, peopled by figures (dignitaries, workers, lovers, travellers) who are fantastic in appearance but recognizable in function. Hence, too, a piece like *Tower*, where the dancers build their own Babel from metal gates fixed together, hang it with their rival flags and eventually find it crashing down in a cataclysmic explosion.

Two motives prompted Nikolais's path of development. He says: 'Modern dance in its traditional sense was an emoted dance; for instance, Graham is as great an actress as she is dancer. I was trying to get down to motion as a basis of the art, not emotion.' And again: 'We were greatly concerned with sex, and I think I disagreed with the idea of the libido as a sexual force dominating and being the only urge of mankind, so I tried first to bring this down to a par level instead of putting neon lights on it all the time.' A possible factor in sparking off these ideas was the puppet theatre for which he worked while studying dance: 'I learned a lot from those puppets. They are all motion and no nerves.'

Nikolais has sometimes been accused of making puppets out of his dancers. After war service and a short, undistinguished dancing career (he was never a 'real dancer, a got-to-move person') he joined the teaching staff at Henry Street Settlement, in New York's Lower East Side, with a small attached theatre situated between a Jewish bakery and a drugstore. He began putting masks on his dancers and using various properties 'at first merely to get them to transcend themselves. The first gesture in art was to remove it from the environment, and they were too much in their own fleshy environment and therefore needed some devices which would take them out of this.'

Having started concealing his dancers with this purely practical motive, however, he 'started also to see the theatre potential of it, so applied myself quite vigorously towards an extension of that'. Consequently, although his dancers sometimes wear ordinary leotards or tights, sometimes they may be draped in long garments which conceal the human shape altogether, or in stretchy sacks giving them the look of a Hepworth statue. Dehumanization, his critics called it, but Nikolais comments that he could not at first understand why: 'I thought I was getting down to basic human-ism. I thought it was rather tragic that man didn't recognize his fellow man when he wasn't on heat, and this rather surprised me.' Certainly his works contain, for all their sometimes abstract appearance, a concern for man in his environment and a liberating humour; he has always had in his company, too, dancers of excep-tional individual gifts, like the small, forceful Phyllis Lamhut, or Murray Louis with his city-slicker charm and fascinating muscular control, permitting solos of minutely detailed movement. Even under completely concealing robes, people of this quality are immediately recognizable.

Yet, although dehumanization is not the right word, Nikolais was working towards something new and startling. He says:

I think that perhaps what I did startled people somewhat, because I began to give more importance to the visual aspects than were customary. In other words, we think of dance as a kinetic art, with everyone getting a hurry on, doing twirls and kicks and so on, but I felt that dance was a visual art; therefore the idea of shapes of things came into our scope as well. Of course, when you have to light, you have to choose there, and I felt that the advent of an arm going through a red light was entirely different from an arm going through a green one, so therefore the colour values could contribute another band of poetry along with the motion. Another thing I tried to find was a form, and in my earlier pieces it took on, to me at any rate, a kind of collage where the pieces exist simultaneously one upon the other. But because of dance being a temporal art they have to be spread out in time instead. I think, for instance, that my *Imago* is really one scene rather than eleven scenes.

Nikolais is his own composer too. His technique is to create a work without accompaniment. Early rehearsals explore various movement possibilities he has in mind for his theme. At this stage 'I don't trust conscious reasoning. I let an idea reflect in and out of my mind for a long time.' Then the work is assembled, section by section. When each is complete, it is rehearsed to find the performance rhythms which will work best. Only then does the composition of the music start. Nowadays the dancers perform and Nikolais runs a blank tape through his tape recorder, marking cues on it by tapping the microphone with a pencil at any change of mood, tempo or action. The score is then composed with a synthesizer which can produce any desired tone. Formerly Nikolais used percussion instruments, but liked to record them on tape, together with other sounds, so that they could be adapted to remove traditional associations. 'I like the idea of sound coming from nowhere, bombarding the ears on its own terms, without the mind associating with the thing that produces it.'

The result may be a work like *Somniloquy* in which bodies in almost constant motion appear and disappear in shifting patches of light and colour. Or *Tent*, a strange ceremony upon, under or within a circular piece of fabric which can lie inert or grow into turreted shapes. It is an art which appeals as much to an ordinary theatrical audience as to a specific dance audience; in fact dance-fans are sometimes rather patronizing about it. When he appeared in Paris, somebody made the joke that the dancers were only there to show off the costumes, and the costumes were only there to show off the lighting.

Yet Nikolais can justify his approach. 'I think that art arises out of the social dynamics which permeate a whole culture, and that culture is apt to have these things spring up at widespread points. I think that only recently have we been able to say things like painting is the art of colour, not cows in the pasture or portraits of dukes and queens. And that music is the art of sound, not of musical instruments, but that we can make music of any sound. I would like that same privilege in dance—as dance is the art of motion I would like to be free to do it in any way possible.'

His concern above all is with 'the magical box of the stage and its illusion. I cannot remember a time, even as a child, when I wasn't involved in transforming something into something else. The word dance is a most generous one, and if you look over history you will find multi-media way back in the early African dances and so on. It was always an act of magic, and I still think today that the artist is the witch doctor and I like to assume that role.'

TWENTIETH CENTURY PACKAGE—FRANCE AND BELGIUM

French dancing has always been beautifully packaged. Even in the austere days immediately after World War II, their designers devised dazzling confections owing almost everything to imagination, since materials were in short supply. This helped establish quickly the promise of young choreographers like Roland Petit and Janine Charrat. Brought up in the individual, idealistic but slightly eccentric tradition of Serge Lifar, who put a heavy French accent on to classical technique, they invented a curious style which combined strong mime and a fluent plastique with flashy use of virtuoso steps. The theatrical elements of their ballets were always notable. Charrat devised a strange work for an all-male cast, 'Adame Miroir, with plot by Genêt: sailors and their mirror-images as symbols of (probably) love and death. Bertrand Castelli devised the theme of Les Algues, in which Charrat showed a man pretending to be mad in order to join his beloved in a lunatic asylum, and eventually becoming mad in fact. In these and other works the production was exceptionally good but the choreography less interesting, although early in her career she had shown herself able in Jeu de Cartes to make a role for Jean Babilée which supremely revealed his mixture of virtuosity and drama.

Petit too failed to find a choreographic expression to match his often brilliant ideas. His effective, straightforward theatrical pieces (notably Carmen, which has been revived in several countries) have always been interspersed with more unusual productions, from the Cocteau Jeune Homme et la Mort, with its lover who proves to be death, and its apotheosis on the rooftops of Paris, through to Paradise Lost which had Nureyev leaping through a giant pair of lips in Martial Raysse's backcloth, and Fonteyn supporting his inverted body in a final pietà. He used a philosophical theme by Jean Cau and pop-art sculpture by Niki de Saint-Phalle for L'Eloge de la Folie; music-hall songs in Ciné-Bijou; giant designs by di Chirico for L'Extase. All the outward marks of experiment are there, and a great many strange inversions of standard technique too, notably a habit of making his dancers lie and wave their legs around, or squat and waggle their backsides at the audience. Yet the total effect is limited because the innovatory elements seem always merely applied to a standard formula.

Other French companies, notably the Contemporary Ballet Theatre founded in the Maison de la Culture at Amiens as a consciously experimental organization, have also been limited in their results by lack of a choreographic tradition or any noted innovation, so that the interest of the ballets has lain most in the designs (by many talented young artists) and the modern music. Nor has France much to show in the way of modern dance.

All this helps to explain the great appeal to French audiences of the ballets of Maurice Béjart, who has his own company in

Brussels (Ballet of the Twentieth Century) and also frequently stages works at the Paris Opéra. Béjart since his early days has made much use of musique concrète, particularly by Pierre Henry. In *Variations for a Door and a Sigh* he adopted a mixture of chance and improvisation, letting the cast draw lots at the beginning to decide who should perform which dances from a sequence chalked up at the back of the stage. Often (as in *Swan* and his version of Stravinsky's *Les Noces*) he employs oriental motifs. His works range from small-scale dance works (like *Erotica*, a duet to Tadeusz Baird's music) to giant arena spectacles sometimes involving actors as well as dancers. Sometimes he gathers a whole group of small works together into a planned programme; not only in an obvious way, like a Stravinsky or (more surprisingly) a Wagner evening, but also for instance a programme based, in intention at least, entirely on experimental work. He has put on an evening in which he created a ballet in public, and on this occasion he and the cast tried at the end to answer the audience's questions by dancing —a process suggesting more courage than communication.

Béjart believes strongly that dance must communicate something to its watchers. He says that 'the renewal of the dance is not an aesthetic problem and passes beyond the world of art. It is concerned with a social question, a spiritual attitude.' He claims from his experience of playing in many different conditions that 'at the same social level, the public has the same reaction throughout the world. If you play to an audience of students, you get the same reactions at the same moment' and the same for a snob audience or one of working men, 'whether it is in Buenos Aires, in Berlin, in London, in Athens, in Tokyo'.

For Béjart, 'dance is a phenomenon of religious origin, and then social, and to the extent that it remains a religious and social phenomenon it fulfils its function. Dance is a rite, sacred and human, and as far as it is a rite it interests me. As a divertissement it is not dance.' He thinks that because Judaism and Christianity separated the flesh from the spirit, and banished dance from the church, dance in the west 'became no more than a worldly entertainment . . . the most affected, empty and conventional of the arts . . . Diaghilev gave it an aesthetic revolution. Now it must undergo an ethical revolution. It must be discovered. This can be achieved through inspiration from other nations where there has been no break in its harmonious development from the first rites. We must disengage essentials common to all nations and races and reunite them in a universal choreography. Dance is a language: primitive, elementary, direct . . .'

Béjart's works arouse fantastic enthusiasm from young audiences convinced that he uniquely holds the secret of a new approach that will give new life to dancing. It is not always easy to agree that his achievements match his aims. Typical works on his Wagner programme were the Venusberg ballet from *Tannhäuser* presented in terms of the men climbing a net to reach the girls hanging in it, but having nothing much to do with them once reached; and *Mathilde*, based on the Wesendonck songs, which involves a singer on stage, some realistic characters in nineteenth-century clothes, some dancers in black tights performing various exercises, and a mysterious man in a leather coat who seems only distantly related to the rest.

Béjart is content for people to interpret his works as they will. He said 'To appreciate a work, you must hold the key. But there are always many possible keys. I try neither to be esoteric nor to make concessions.' He remains on the one hand fond of classical dancing: his *Prospectives* programme began with dancers performing exercises at the barre, and *Ni fleurs, ni couronnes* is a set of variations on themes from *The Sleeping Beauty*. At the other extreme are his big spectaculars (one to Beethoven's Ninth Symphony, one to the Berlioz *Romeo and Juliet*) involving massed casts, violent effects and an underlying attitude very much in sympathy with the young people who throng his audiences. Love, peace and revolution are his themes, and on this depends much of his success. His theories are admirable, his gifts as a producer immense. If he had a choreographic talent to match he would leave most of his rivals far behind. As it is, he says, 'the important thing is not reaching perfection, but striving to achieve something.'

A ZEST FOR DANCE—PAUL TAYLOR

When Paul Taylor was asked to contribute an essay to a book on modern dance, he offered a piece called 'Down with choreography' which began 'A lot of dance writers, it seems, neglect to write about what most people notice first when they go to see dancing . . . It is time more should be said about the dancer.' Although an exceptionally interesting choreographer, and one of the few who can be really funny in movement when he wishes, Taylor disclaims any knowledge or theories: 'Me?' he will say, 'I don't know anything about choreography, I only know how to make things for dancers to do.'

He will explain any work in his repertory by suggesting, for instance, that at the time he made it they needed a lyrical ballet ('Everybody knows what "lyric" means—long arms' says Taylor in a deflating aside) or thought it would be interesting to make a really unpleasant work, one to evoke the nasty taste you sometimes wake up with in the mornings. He also insists that his main purpose is to make good roles for himself and the other members of the company.

In fact he has a clear idea what he is doing, and wrote in a programme note: 'These dances are primarily meant to be a kind of food for the eye. If they evoke dramatic images and riddles, the key to their solution lies not so much in the brain, but in the senses and the eye of the spectator. It was not my intention to present literary messages, although certain dances here have as their focal point a common subject with certain writings. But still, my "message", as Humphrey Bogart once said, "is nothing you could send by Western Union".'

For all his disarming denial of theories, Taylor is one of the most important practitioners of contemporary American dance and has contributed notably to its development. His earliest works were the most obviously experimental in form. In one of them, *Duet*, he stood and Toby Glanternik sat on the stage, both of them motionless, for three minutes. There was no music and the only action was that of a fan which provided a breeze. In these early days Taylor collaborated with Robert Rauschenberg; the sole surviving manifestation of their work together is *3 Epitaphs*, in which Rauschenberg covered the dancers completely (face, hands and all) in tight black costumes set with pieces of mirror which flashed light reflections about the stage and towards the audience. Taylor's choreography (which began as a very long piece but was cut down by him to only a few minutes before he was satisfied) is a zany cross between wild farce and macabre ghoulishness, with overtones of black-face vaudeville shows as well, set to early American brass-band music of extremely syncopated raucousness.

Taylor's attitude to music is in some ways off-hand. *Scudorama* was rehearsed to Stravinsky's *Rite of Spring*, but performed to a score specially written by C. Jackson. *From Sea to Shining Sea* was first danced to Charles Ives's 'Three Places in New England' but when copyright difficulties arose John Herbert McDowell composed a new score for it. Yet Taylor created also the beautiful *Aureole* to pieces by Handel, one of the most perfect of plotless ballets to classic music; to Haydn's 'Seven Last Words' he made first the radiantly lovely *Duet* and later a longer abstract work *Lento*; and he even successfully set a two-act ballet, *Orbs*, to Beethoven's last quartets.

One section of this ballet is in the form of a comic interlude in modern dress; this has a clear story about a wedding rehearsal and ceremony, and subsequently a harvest festival celebration. This is only the scherzo, however, to the big four-part symphonic structure of the ballet as a whole. The rest of *Orbs* has a very detailed programme but very little explicit narrative. It is concerned with the sun and planets, the rotation of the heavens and the seasons; it is also, by implication, about religion and society, man's relations with his god (or gods) and his fellow men.

None of this is handled literally. The performers are named in the programme as appearing 'for' (not 'as') the sun, planets and moons. Taylor himself is the central figure (the sun) throughout, either in white flecked with glittering patches, or as the priest in the terrestrial sequences. He teaches the planets to make love; he is angry with them when they go their own ways; when he withdraws from them they sink in wintry gloom. Each sequence has clear emotional qualities which are unambiguous; the intellectual meaning ascribed to them is largely a matter for the spectator, and the more layers of significance you can take in simultaneously, the richer the ballet appears. (Besides the meanings I have already suggested, it is neither difficult nor far-fetched to read the work as a—perhaps unintended—autobiography, an allegory of a choreographer's relationships with his dancers of whom he has said 'my company is my family'.) Equally, the dancing is capable of enjoyment without interpretation, combining elements of many different styles developed by Taylor for his shorter works into one epic form.

Other works by Taylor have tended to be more enigmatic in their meaning than *Orbs*. Sometimes this is simply because no meaning is intended. One British critic asked Taylor the meaning of two balls which roll across the stage in his collage-ballet *Public Domain*, and was told 'They don't mean anything; we just thought they would be amusing.' Which they were. In *Private Domain*, however, there was clearly a meaning hinted at immediately by the décor, a framework across the front of the stage allowing the audience to see only through three cut-out sections, each framed in a dull surround. This reliance on design is something rare in Taylor's ballets; his practice is to finish a work and then give the designer a free hand: 'Just let them see the dance as many times as they like, answer their questions, and leave them to work it out in their own way. The trick is to select the right designer for the right dance.' The painter who has most often worked with him lately is Alex Katz; generally he creates abstract patterns of colour on the dancers' tights, but for *Private Domain* he put them in pale briefs like swimwear or underwear. The first effect, seen through the triple proscenium frame, is that the stage picture is very much like a modern painting with figures; later a sense of voyeurism grows from the combination of having to peer through a frame at these partly dressed figures and also from the choreography itself, which involves all the performers but one in games or activities where they touch each other, while the one (Taylor) moves carefully among them with his hand held slightly out at the angle of a man anxious not to be jostled in a crowd.

Yet the dances can again be viewed purely on the level of a movement spectacle, the proscenium frame being taken as a device to ensure selective viewing of just certain angles or groupings which will vary according to where you sit. In all Taylor's works, the most involved as well as the simplest, the first motivating force is the zest for dancing. This makes him in some respects more akin to the classical ballet tradition although his work is based on a modern dance technique; and he names Balanchine (who used him as a soloist in the classical, non-Graham section of *Episodes*) and Tudor as well as Graham and Cunningham in acknowledging the 'aggravating and inescapable debt I owe to my teachers and mentors'. Yet what he prizes most in his dance inheritance is 'the licence which American dance has given me: the freedom to do whatever kinds of dances I feel are worth doing'.

FROM BOTH SIDES—RUSSIA AND THE USA: RECENT DEVELOPMENTS

Compared with the experiments of the 1920s, modern Soviet ballet seems very staid. This is generally attributed to an official policy of encouraging only such art as can easily be understood by a wide public, and that must be a factor. Another part of the explanation however is a reaction against the earlier experiments, and also the fact that the latest generation of choreographers seems temperamentally inclined towards a classical approach anyway. As what they see of western ballet is mostly companies such as the Royal Ballet, New York City Ballet and the Paris Opéra Ballet, they probably find it difficult (given some natural differences of taste) to understand western suggestions that their own works are out of touch with modern trends.

Since the monumental productions of Leonid Lavrovsky (with *Romeo and Juliet* the best known and the best), which carried Fokine's theories as far as they could go, his successor at the Bolshoi has emphasized classical technique. Yuri Grigorovich (like most of his western contemporaries) has staged new versions of the Petipa classics; his have put even the old character dances on point. In *Legend of Love* he used elements of oriental styles but converted these into a variant of the classical technique, and in *Spartacus* he has even an ancient Roman orgy taking place with the girls in blocked ballet shoes. The success of *Spartacus* is owed mainly to the stirring virtuoso dances for the men; partly also to the vivid, larger-than-life characterizations of the four opposed leading roles. In establishing these characters, a purely formal device plays an important part, when at the end of most scenes a drop-curtain descends and one character is left alone on stage for a danced soliloquy, corresponding in its emotional effect to a close-up in the cinema.

Grigorovich sees that 'there can exist, must exist, dance form without subject matter, like the symphonic dance. However, I have never myself worked in this form, and inasmuch as I work in the theatre, I am interested in the theatrical aspect . . . The whole effect interests me. So that I am really for a form of ballet theatre which would have a literary content as well as dance.' Yet he insists that 'pure dance always exists when you are choreographing anything'. As the principal influence on his work he names Lopukhov who 'had a great creative achievement. He knows the classic ballets exceedingly well . . . When he restored a number of old ballets, he had the talent to do it in their appropriate style, so that you couldn't tell the difference . . . On the other hand he also did very experimental work in the '20s . . . but because his experiments were so extreme the ballets were not successful.'

Grigorovich says that 'all the younger choreographers of this generation have tried to take as much as possible' from Lopukhov; and even the older Konstantin Sergeyev in his ballets similarly emphasized the classical dancing for conveying his plots. Oleg

Vinogradov, whose success with a company in remote Novosibirsk led to commissions from the Bolshoi and Kirov, works on similar lines.

Turning from Russia to the United States, you might expect to find a very different state of affairs. Yet (doubtless from different motives) the young generation of American ballet choreographers also mostly follow strictly classical lines. New York City Ballet has shown a few works by a number of other choreographers than Balanchine (although the old master has always completely dominated the repertory) among whom John Taras, Jacques d'Amboise and John Clifford have had a measure of success—all working in their own variants of the Balanchine pure-dance manner, with the youngest of them, Clifford, holding out most hope of finding a personal language within that manner.

The rival major company, American Ballet Theatre, has consciously tried to give chances to aspiring choreographers, both with special workshop performances and the opportunity to create works for the repertory. In Eliot Feld they developed a notable talent until he left to form his own company. Since then others have had at least a measure of success, Michael Smuin with *Pulcinella Variations*, Dennis Nahat with *Brahms Quintet*: both lively pure-dance works. Even Alvin Ailey, whose main involvement is with modern dance in his own successful American Dance Theatre (based primarily on Negro traditions—spirituals, blues and jazz) has turned more than once to create works with a classical technique for ballet dancers, including *The River* for Ballet Theatre to a score specially written by Duke Ellington. In this work he managed even to suggest something of the problem of America's two nations in pure dance, with a white and a Negro soloist working on opposite sides of the stage separated by a seething mass of bodies between.

With Eliot Feld, the mixture of techniques comes in again. He danced in ballets by Balanchine, Robbins, Tudor and others, and in the modern dance companies of Pearl Lang, Sophie Maslow and Donald McKayle. His first work, *Harbinger*, was a playful set of dances to Prokofiev music, created bit by bit, at first just for his own satisfaction. Then in *At Midnight* (to Mahler's Rückert songs) he made a strongly emotional piece, with the loneliness of the soloists heightened by the couples passing by, and with a strange prologue in which one man is tormented by a dark shadowy group who keep pulling him back. Yet the drama here is completely non-specific. Before forming his own American Ballet Company, Feld said he would like a repertory embracing works as diverse as Balanchine's *Apollo* and Graham's *Primitive Mysteries*; he has in fact presented in addition to his own creations ballets by McKayle and Herbert Ross (*The Maids*, based on Genêt, with the title parts played by men) and a revival of Fokine's *Carnaval*.

He says that 'a dancer's body is his instrument, and I think that just as a musician should be able to play Bach and Bartók, so ideally a dancer should be able to dance Petipa and Graham. Whether or not this is entirely possible we shall see. I think that in America we stand some kind of chance of moving in these different areas because of what we have been exposed to . . . Obviously you need talent and also dedicated dancers, but I am sure it is possible.'

Also much concerned with the dancer's body as his instrument, although in a different context, is Robert Joffrey, director of the City Center Joffrey Ballet in New York. He says 'I once saw Mr Balanchine spend half an hour showing someone how to smile. This is the kind of detail that pays dividends. It is amazing how much you can develop the individual dancer, but that dancer must be given individual attention. You see, bodies vary so vastly, and yet the general patterns of our ballet classes are based upon the ideal body. How many ideal bodies do you come across?'

His company also has a diverse repertory; initially with works largely by Balanchine and by the resident choreographer Gerald Arpino, later with the admixture of many different kinds of work, including some big-scale Diaghilev revivals (*Petrushka* and *The Three Cornered Hat*) and others ranging from Bournonville's classic dance work *Konservatoriet* to Jooss's *Green Table*, taking in also lighthearted works by Ashton and Cranko and contributions from some far less talented producers. Arpino's contributions to the repertory are in many different moods, filling the company's needs from time to time. At the one extreme are exuberant show-off works like *Viva Vivaldi!* or a lyrical duet like *Sea Shadow*; at the other, a work like *Clowns* which makes an allegory of a man's condition from white-clad figures, giant balloons, white objects plopping from the sky and an enormous transparent bag which at the end rises at the back and ingests the performers.

Joffrey himself is responsible for the work which has won the most sensational success, *Astarte*. This uses an acid rock group, and projected pictures of the dancers which zoom, merge, expand, multiply or sink again; even brightly coloured searchlights blinking into the audience. One of the two dancers starts sitting in the audience, rises as if in a trance to walk on stage, strip to a single white garment and dance with the girl (decorated with oriental patterning on her forehead and her white tights) who is already there. At the end the man goes out at the back and, in a film, is seen (still nearly naked) walking out through the garage behind the theatre, ignored by the motorists there. The ballet is in effect the application of discotheque methods (loud frenzied music, varying lights and films on uneven surfaces) and a startling prologue and epilogue to what is otherwise an ordinary although sexy duet. Its strength and weakness are both summed up in Clive Barnes's comment after the première: '*Astarte* is a trip.'

OUTSIDE IN

The very first concert of dance by the Judson Dance Theater included a piece with choreography by the composer John Herbert
McDowell, several others in which he appeared and one for which
the painter Alex Hay was joint choreographer. Another artist,
Robert Morris, contributed to the fourth programme and Robert
Rauschenberg soon afterwards. At the same time as people like
these were coming into dance, the dance itself and related activities
were occasionally moving into the great world outside. There was
for instance the *Timetable Piece* by George Brecht in which John
Cage's entire composition class went to Grand Central Station and
interpreted the figures in the timetables to establish various actions
they were to perform on the spot. Steve Paxton invented *Afternoon*, a 'concert in the forest' which was given at Berkley Heights,
New Jersey; and Brecht's *Motor Vehicle Sundown Event* was performed by a great number of automobiles also in New Jersey.

Meanwhile at Judson more or less anyone who happened to turn
up to meetings of the group was sucked into their activities.
Dancers who had previously been performers only began to do
choreography (Judith Dunn was one such) and laymen were used
as performers. McDowell recorded that the activity at Judson,
'although it was dance, it always included painters, sometimes
writers, three composers that I know of off hand, and all of these
people danced and choreographed. And these people coming from
other fields brought not simply new dance ideas but whole new
concepts of what dance was. Or could be. Which was the upsetting
and stimulating factor.'

As early as 1952 Cage had presented, at Black Mountain College,
North Carolina, the first of his theatre pieces, with Cage reading
a lecture from the upper rungs of a ladder, Cunningham dancing,
David Tudor playing the piano, two poets reading their works in
turn, Rauschenberg playing scratchy records on an old phono-
graph (and some of his white paintings hung overhead) while two
other people projected movies and still pictures on the walls.

During the 1960s other people began to stage happenings,
largely under Cage's influence at first. Jack Kaprow and Robert
Whitman were prominent in this movement; one of Kaprow's first
productions was at Judson and involved Jim Dine and Claes
Oldenburg.

Robert Morris created and took part in many dances, both at
Judson and elsewhere; the choreographer James Waring described
him as 'one of the very few painters and sculptors who could perform. His attention is very much in what he's doing and he's
terribly relaxed and everything is very focused and serene and very
clearly projected in terms of his intention. Which is just not true for
instance of Rauschenberg, who is a kind of Mortimer Snerd of the
dance. I don't mean his theatrical ideas, which are often marvelous. But he's not a good performer whereas Bob Morris is.'

1   Isadora Duncan *Pan and Echo* (dance without music)
     Drawing by Valentine Lecompte

Kurt Jooss *The Green Table* (Fritz Cohen) 1932
Max Zomosa as Death, Michael Uthoff as the Standard
Bearer in New York City Center Joffrey Ballet revival

3 Jean Börlin *Relâche* (Erik Satie) 1924
Les Ballets Suédois in Picabia's setting for act 2

4 Art Bauman *Burlesque/Black and White* 1967
Bauman with students at The Place

5   Taller de Montevideo
Chronus I (mixed-media event) 1969

6   Taller de Montevideo
     Chronus II (mixed-media event) 1969

7   Geoff Moore
Accumulator (mixed-media event) revised version 1970
Moving Being: Brian Hibbard, John Carter

8   Geoff Moore *Window* (mixed-media dance) 1969
     Moving Being: Julie Witford, Robin Courbet

9   Alfredo Rodriguez Arias *Dracula* (play with music and dance) 1969
     TSE Company: Marucha Bo, Facundo Bo, Juan Stoppani

10   Bronislava Nijinska *Les Noces* (Igor Stravinsky) 1923
         Royal Ballet revival

11   *Les Noces*

12   George Balanchine *Episodes* (Anton Webern) 1959
New York City Ballet

13   George Balanchine *Four Temperaments* (Paul Hindemith) 1946
New York City Ballet: Arthur Mitchell

15   Martha Graham *Night Journey* (William Schuman) 1947
      Graham, Stuart Hodes

16   Martha Graham *Clytemnestra* (Halim El-Dabh) 1958
      Graham, David Wood

17   Martha Graham *Acrobats of God* (Carlos Surinach) 1960

18   Martha Graham *Seraphic Dialogue* (Norman Dello Joio) 1955
Ethel Winter, Linda Hodes, Helen McGehee, Yuriko

21　　Jerome Robbins *New York Export, Opus Jazz* (Robert Prince) 1958
　　　Ballets: USA

22　　Jerome Robbins *Dances at a Gathering* (Frederic Chopin) 1969
　　　Revival by the Royal Ballet: Laura Connor, Ann Jenner, David
　　　Wall, Rudolf Nureyev, Anthony Dowell

23   Merce Cunningham

24   Merce Cunningham *Variations V* (John Cage) 1965
      John Cage, David Tudor, Gordon Mumma in foreground

25   Merce Cunningham *Place* (Gordon Mumma) 1966
Cunningham (on floor, right) and Dance Company

26   Merce Cunningham *How to Pass, Kick, Fall and Run* (John Cage)
1965 Cunningham

27   Merce Cunningham *RainForest* (David Tudor) 1968
Cunningham

29   *Canfield*

30 Merce Cunningham *Second Hand* (John Cage) 1970
Carolyn Brown, Cunningham

31 Merce Cunningham *Scramble* (Toshi Ichiyanagi) 1967
Cunningham and Dance Company

32   Merce Cunningham *Signals* (Tudor-Mumma-Cage) 1970
Valda Setterfield, Douglas Dunn, Mel Wong

33   Merce Cunningham *Tread* (Christian Wolff) 1970
      Jeff Slayton, Sandra Neels

34   Merce Cunningham *Walkaround Time* (David Behrman) 1968
      Cunningham and Dance Company

35   Antony Tudor *Shadowplay* (Charles Koechlin) 1967
      The Royal Ballet: Merle Park, Anthony Dowell

36   *Shadowplay*
Anthony Dowell, Derek Rencher

37   Kenneth MacMillan *Song of the Earth* (Gustav Mahler) 1965
Stuttgart Ballet: Egon Madsen, Marcia Haydée

38   Frederick Ashton *Marguerite and Armand* (Franz Liszt), 1963
Margot Fonteyn, Rudolf Nureyev

39   John Cranko *The Interrogation* (Bernd Alois Zimmermann) 1967
     Stuttgart Ballet: Egon Madsen and group

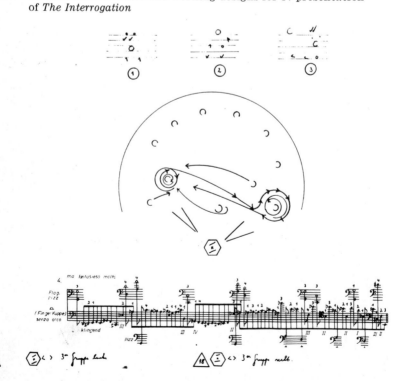

40   Zimmermann's music and working designs for TV presentation
     of *The Interrogation*

41   Peter Darrell *Houseparty* (Francis Poulenc) 1964
Western Theatre Ballet: Sylvia Wellman

42   Peter Darrell *Home* (Béla Bartók) 1965
Western Theatre Ballet

43   Peter Darrell *Herodiade* (Paul Hindemith) 1970
Scottish Theatre Ballet: Elaine McDonald

44   Alwin Nikolais *Imago* (Nikolais) 1963

45   Alwin Nikolais *Tower* (Nikolais) 1968

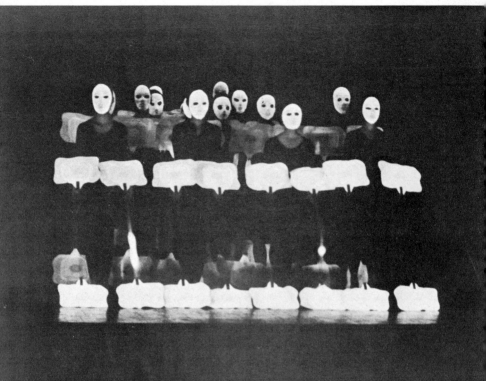

48   Alwin Nikolais *Somniloquy* (Nikolais) 1967

Opposite

46   Alwin Nikolais *Galaxy* (Nikolais) 1965

47   Alwin Nikolais *Allegory* (Nikolais) 1959

c

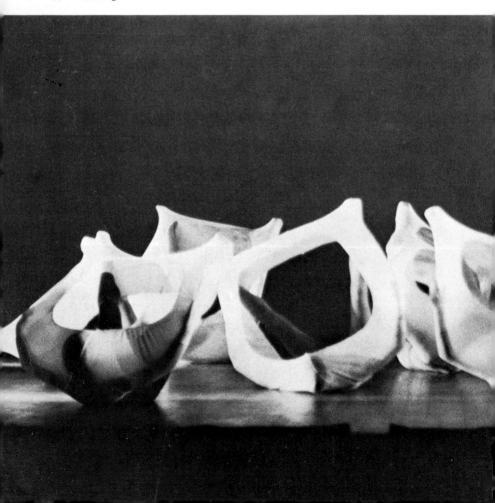

51   Alwin Nikolais *Sanctum* (Nikolais) 1964

Maurice Béjart *The Rite of Spring* (Igor Stravinsky) 1959
Rudolf Nureyev

56   Paul Taylor *Orbs* (Ludwig van Beethoven) 1966
Taylor and company

58 Eliot Feld *At Midnight* (Gustav Mahler) 1967
American Ballet Company

59 Robert Joffrey *Astarte* (The Crome Syrcus) 1967
City Center Joffrey Ballet: Nancy Robinson, Christian Holder

63   Kenneth King *Blow-Out* 1966
Laura Dean, Kenneth King

64   Twyla Tharp *Group Activities* (dance without music) 1969
Working charts by the choreographer

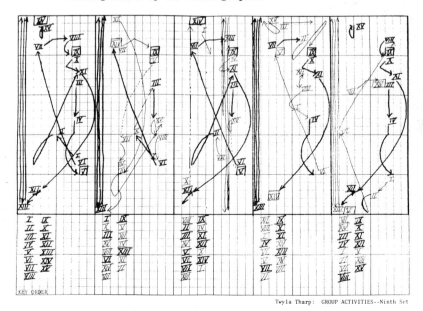

Twyla Tharp: GROUP ACTIVITIES--Ninth Set

65   Rudi van Dantzig *Moments* (Anton Webern) 1968
      Dutch National Ballet

66   Rudi van Dantzig *Monument for a Dead Boy* (Jan Boerman) 1965
      Dutch National Ballet: Toer van Schayk

67   Rudi van Dantzig *Epitaphs* (György Ligeti) 1969
Dutch National Ballet: Guus Wijnoogst, Toer van Schayk

68   *Epitaphs* Guus Wijnoogst, Charlotte Sprangers, Christine
Anthony, Toer van Schayk

70   Hans van Manen *Situation* (sounds for amateur film-makers) 1970
        Netherlands Dance Theatre: Jon Benoit, Anja Licher

71   Hans van Manen *Twice* (pop music) 1970
        Netherlands Dance Theatre

72   Hans van Manen *Solo for Voice 1* (John Cage) 1968
Netherlands Dance Theatre: Anne Haenen, Hans Knill, Susan Kenniff

73   Glen Tetley *Pierrot Lunaire* (Arnold Schoenberg) 1962
Revival by Ballet Rambert: Christopher Bruce

74　Glen Tetley *Freefall* (Max Schubel) 1967
Revival by Ballet Rambert: Sandra Craig, Marilyn Williams,
Bob Smith, Gayrie MacSween, Christopher Bruce

75　Glen Tetley *Sargasso* (Ernst Krenek) 1964
Netherlands Dance Theatre: Willy de la Bije, Jaap Flier

79   Glen Tetley *Circles* (Luciano Berio) 1968
Netherlands Dance Theatre: Willy de la Bije

Opposite

77   Glen Tetley *Mythical Hunters* (Oedeon Partos) 1966
Revival by Netherlands Dance Theatre: Marianne Sarstädt

78   Glen Tetley *Arena* (Morton Subotnick) 1969
Netherlands Dance Theatre: Frans Vervenne, Jaap Flier

81   John Chesworth *Pawn to King 5* (The Pink Floyd) 1968
      Ballet Rambert

80   Norman Morrice *Blindsight* (Bob Downes) 1969
      Ballet Rambert: Jonathan Taylor, Sandra Craig, Mary Prestidge,
      Susan Cooper

82   John Chesworth *Time Base* (Witold Lutoslawski) 1966
Ballet Rambert

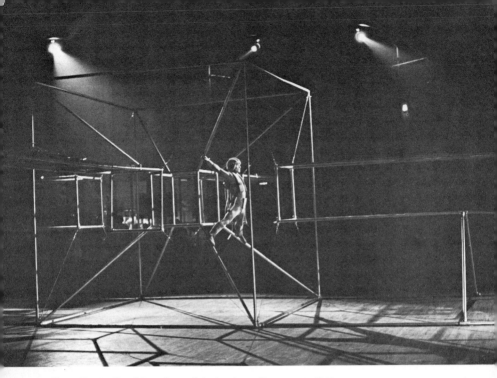

83   Peter Dockley *Spaced* (mixed-media event) 1969

84   Peter Dockley *Never Never Land* (mixed-media event) 1970
      Netherlands Dance Theatre

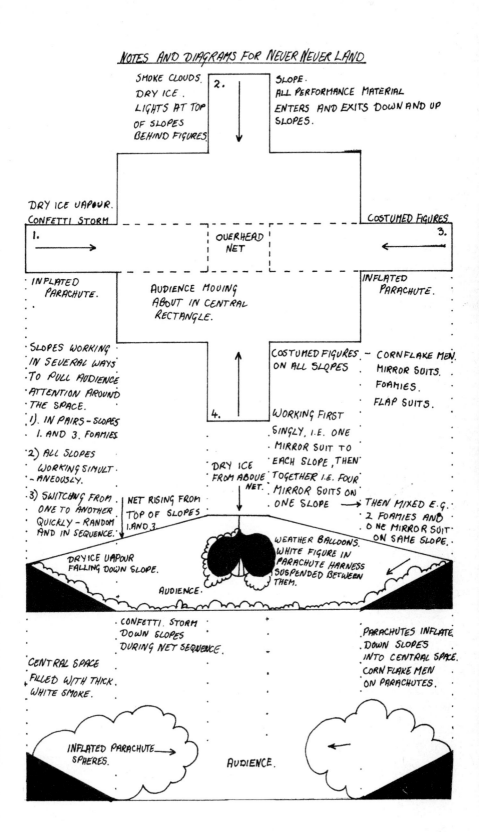

NOTES AND DIAGRAMS FOR NEVER NEVER LAND

SMOKE CLOUDS.
DRY ICE.
LIGHTS AT TOP
OF SLOPES
BEHIND FIGURES.

2.

SLOPE.
ALL PERFORMANCE MATERIAL
ENTERS AND EXITS DOWN AND UP
SLOPES.

DRY ICE VAPOUR.
CONFETTI STORM

COSTUMED FIGURES

1.

OVERHEAD
NET

3.

INFLATED
PARACHUTE.

AUDIENCE MOVING
ABOUT IN CENTRAL
RECTANGLE.

INFLATED
PARACHUTE.

· SLOPES WORKING ·
IN SEVERAL WAYS
· TO PULL AUDIENCE
· ATTENTION AROUND ·
· THE SPACE. ·
1). IN PAIRS — SLOPES
· 1. AND 3. FOAMIES.

· 2) ALL SLOPES
· WORKING SIMULT·
· — ANEOUSLY.

· 3) SWITCHING FROM ·
ONE TO ANOTHER
QUICKLY — RANDOM
AND IN SEQUENCE.

COSTUMED FIGURES ·
ON ALL SLOPES

4.

WORKING FIRST
· SINGLY, I.E. ONE
· MIRROR SUIT TO
· EACH SLOPE, THEN
TOGETHER I.E. FOUR
· MIRROR SUITS ON ·
· ONE SLOPE

— CORNFLAKE MEN.
MIRROR SUITS.
FOAMIES.
FLAP SUITS.

→ THEN MIXED E.G. ·
· 2 FOAMIES AND ·
· ONE MIRROR SUIT ·
ON SAME SLOPE.

· DRY ICE
FROM ABOVE
NET.

· NET RISING FROM
TOP OF SLOPES
1. AND 3.

DRY ICE VAPOUR
FALLING DOWN SLOPE.

AUDIENCE.

WEATHER BALLOONS.
WHITE FIGURE IN
PARACHUTE HARNESS
SUSPENDED BETWEEN
THEM.

· CONFETTI. STORM ·
DOWN SLOPES
DURING NET SEQUENCE.

·PARACHUTES INFLATE.
·DOWN SLOPES
INTO CENTRAL SPACE.
CORN FLAKE MEN
ON PARACHUTES.

·CENTRAL SPACE
·FILLED WITH THICK.
WHITE SMOKE.

INFLATED PARACHUTE
SPHERES.

AUDIENCE.

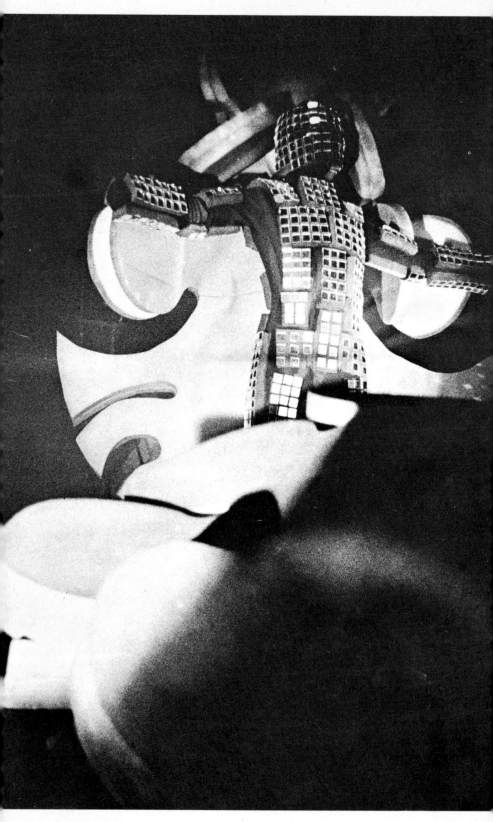

87   Pavel Smok *Gangrene* (Charlie Mingus) 1967
Studio Ballet Prague

Birgit Cullberg *Eurydice is dead* (Morricone and Pontecorno) 1968
Cullberg Ballet: Niklas Ek, Lena Wennergren

89 Pauline de Groot *Rainmakers* (Floris Rommerts) 1968
    De Groot (right) and group

90 Richard Alston *Nowhere Slowly* (Stockhausen) 1970
    London Contemporary Dance Company: Kiki Obermer

by Peter Maxwell Davies
in collaboration with William Louther

Solo Cello: Jennifer Ward Clarke
Solo Dancer: William Louther

(for Jennifer Ward Clarke and William Louther)

VESALII ICONES
(Andreas Vesalius—
De Humani Corporis Fabrica
1543)

for Cello Solo, small instrumental group, and Dancer

1 *Prima musculorum tabula* The agony in the garden.
2 *Secunda musculorum tabula* The betrayal of Judas.
3 *Tertia musculorum tabula* Christ and Pilate.
4 *Quarta musculorum tabula.* The flagellation.
5 *Quinta musculorum tabula.* Christ condemned to death.
6 *Sexta musculorum tabula.* The mocking of Christ.
7 *Septima musculorum tabula.* Christ receives the Cross.
8 *Octava musculorum tabula.* St. Veronica wipes His face.
9 *Nona musculorum tabula.* Christ prepared for death.
10 *Decima musculorum tabula.* Christ nailed to the Cross.
11 *Undecima musculorum tabula.* The death of Christ.
12 *Duodecima musculorum tabula.* The descent from the Cross.
13 *Decimatertia tabula.* The entombment of Christ.
14 *Decimaquarta musculorum tabula.* The Resurrection—Antichrist.

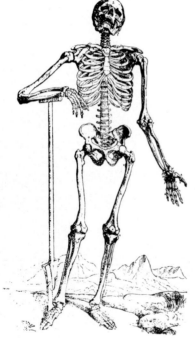

The idea of eventually making a set of fourteen dances, based on the illustrations to Vesalius, came to me when I bought a facsimile edition of the 'de Humani Corporis Fabrica' two years ago; the idea of superposing the Vesalius images on the fourteen stations of the Cross (slightly modified to include the Resurrection) came much later, and was the direct stimulus to composing the work.

In 'St. Thomas Wake—Foxtrot for Orchestra', I had worked with three levels of musical experience—that of the original sixteenth century 'St. Thomas Wake' pavan, played on the harp, the level of the foxtrots derived from this, played by a foxtrot band, and the level of my "real" music, also derived from the pavan, played by the symphony orchestra. These three levels interacted on each other—a visual image of the effect would be three glass sheets spaced parallel a small distance apart, with the three musical "styles" represented on them, so that when one's eye focuses from the front on to one sheet, its perception is modified by the marks on the other glass sheets, to which one's focus will be distracted, and therefore constantly changing.

In the 'Vesalii Icones', such processes are not only present in the music, but, more importantly, the Dancer has a parallel set of superpositions—(1) the Vesalius illustrations, (2) the stations of the Cross, and (3) his own body. (In the music, there are three levels—plainsong, "popular" music, and my *own* music derived from the other two, but the three are very much fused, and clearly separate identities emerge rarely).

91   William Louther *Vesalii Icones* (Peter Maxwell Davies) 1969
      Pierrot Players: Page from Programme note by Maxwell Davies
      with drawing by Andreas Vesalius, 1543

Rauschenberg's activities, however, influenced modern dance a lot because of his function as artistic director of the Cunningham company. In *Story* he not only found the costumes and improvised the setting, but at least sometimes appeared on stage. At the company's London première he walked on carrying a large stuffed eagle; for the next few nights he made an entrance to dye and hang up some cloths on stage; then he spent four consecutive performances constructing a combine painting on stage. Rauschenberg presumably influenced Cunningham towards the more spontaneous sort of choreography, dictated partly by the specific environment of the performance, which was his own ideal, manifested for instance in the 1963 Pop Art Festival in Washington where Rauschenberg and the Swedish sculptor P. O. Ultveldt, wearing roller skates and huge spoked sails made from parachutes, swooped round a skating rink with Carolyn Brown in Rauschenberg's *Pelican*. Another production of his, *The Construction of Boston*, was given at the Maidman Playhouse, New York, with Viola Farber and Steve Paxton (from Cunningham's company) going through the routines of an ordinary day, which included being rained upon by an elaborate sprinkler, while the Swiss sculptor Jean Tinguely built a wall of cinder blocks between them and the audience which, when completed, effectively completed the show too.

For a while the dancers and painters were experimenting on parallel lines which later separated. The spectacular climax of the involvement of painters in movement activity came with *Nine Evenings: Theatre and Engineering* presented at the 69th Regiment Armory in New York in October 1966, with a mixed cast of painters, dancers, composers and scientists. The theatre and the engineering were sometimes rather remotely connected. In Alex Hay's *Grass Field* the painter-choreographer distributed two piles of large numbered sheets over the floor area; his face was then projected on a giant television screen while Paxton and Rauschenberg systematically sorted them again into two piles. Rauschenberg's *Open Score* began with a couple playing tennis with prepared racquets which at each stroke emitted a ping and a short radio transmission which switched off some of the arena lights. When all were out, the match ended, and in the second half of the work a large crowd performed exercises in the dark, being projected on television screens by means of sensitivity cameras and infra-red rays.

Some of the other events of the series were more spectacular. Robert Whitman's *Two Holes of Water* for instance included gunfire, flashing lights, cars and vans, coloured movies and black and white television as well as live action. Unfortunately, quite apart from the rather strained conception of some contributions, the technology during the evenings had a habit of breaking down too often for comfort.

I

JUDSON AND AFTER

The activities that developed among the group of dancers and others associated with Judson Dance Theater in the 1960s, especially in the first couple of years from summer 1962, had a marvellously liberating effect on the young generation of American modern dancers. Their predecessors, with much painful effort, had established a technique, a repertory and a tradition, against which the youngsters revolted with as much enthusiasm as the older generation had once shown in overturning the classical ballet.

Under the influence of John Cage's iconoclastic theories, incited by the dance composition courses of James Waring and of Robert and Judith Dunn, and spurred on by the simultaneous development of 'happenings' which abandoned all conventional ideas of theatre, the Judson group felt free to try anything. Judith Dunn commented:

As a teacher Bob Dunn was outrageous. He allowed interminable rambling discussion, which often strayed wildly from the opening point. He permitted class members to deal with whatever hit their fancy. To examine, consider and present any object, dance, collection of words, sounds and what have you in answer to the problems he had given for study. He posed questions arising out of the most basic elements—structure, method, material. He was in one respect persistent . . . evaluation, in terms of 'good or bad', 'acceptable—rejected', were eliminated from discussion and analysis replaced them . . . There was no formula to be filled. Initially this caused some anxiety. What he asked was that invention take place and that work continue to be produced economically and practically.

The dances in consequences could be of all types. Judith Dunn's *Dew Horse* began with her entering with a figure of a pigeon held between her teeth. After some staccato movements and pauses she crumpled on the ground in a foetal position and released the bird. Repetition of a similar process followed. There was no accompaniment except the sound of the dancer's movements. In Yvonne Rainer's *We Shall Run*, eleven people did just that to music from the Berlioz Requiem. Steve Paxton and Yvonne Rainer did *Word Words*; first a long solo (about seven minutes) for her, while he leaned against the wall; then a solo for him which in time the audience could realize was in fact the same solo, while she leaned on the wall; and finally both of them repeating it simultaneously. Reportedly because this lasted more than twenty minutes and they were afraid people might be bored, they decided to wear just G-strings and, for her, pasties.

Miss Rainer's *3 Satie Spoons* consisted of balances, arm folding and similar activities accompanied by the *Gymnopédies*, and at the end some cheerful cheeping noises and a comment that 'the grass is greener where the sun is yellower'. In *Three Seascapes* she first ran round the stage wearing a coat, sometimes falling full-length without removing her hands from her pockets, to music from Rachmaninoff's Second Piano Concerto. Then to LaMonte Young's 'Poem for Chairs, Table, Benches' (played by scraping their legs on the floor) she cautiously made a slow diagonal progress across the performing area before laying a piece of chiffon and the coat on the floor. Finally, while screaming, she rolled in and out of these objects, hurling them around her and kicking in the air; then just stood up and turned her head to the left.

Some *Thoughts on Improvisation* which she has on occasion included in her dance concerts explain some of the thoughts behind her work:

I think the impulse comes first.
So I keep on sizing up the situation, see, and I make decisions.
I will not make an issue of it.
I can choose not to obey an impulse.
Anyway the thing is, I don't have to do any of it.
I choose to do this, I choose to play the game this way.
One must take a chance on the fitness of one's own instincts.
One must take a risk of acting as though no other possibility exists.
Loaded with expectancy, a sphere for action, what more could one wish for?

But equally she could be marvellously deflating. Asked whether she and Robert Morris had really appeared nude in an 8-minute duet she replied 'Oh no, we both wore a light coating of baby oil.' And the spoken accompaniment to *Corridor Solo* began with the remark 'I want to make a piece about sleep,' went on about sleep and sleeplessness, your own bed and other people's, where and when and with whom, leaving the spectator concentrating hard on her quiet, simple movements in case he was missing the connexion, only to end with the remark 'I want to make a dance about sleep. Some day I will make a dance about sleeping. Not right now.'

Yvonne Rainer was only part of Judson, although by general consent one of the more innovatory participants. There were also, besides those already mentioned, many others; their activities included a striptease, a dance with a film projector strapped to the dancer's back, a dance with ironing and slow-motion hairbrushing, a dancer followed and illuminated by a motorbike, a love scene climbing into a hammock, a Spanish dance in drag, a duet where the dancers wore radios at their waists, tuned to different stations, turning the volume up and down at intervals. Anything was possible. Judith Dunn said 'This is one of the most important things about the Judson, that they made very good use of history, opened up into dance, allowed all kinds of other things to enter as material.' And McDowell: 'This point about the mixing of non-dance people into a dance thing. It's not so much the idea of making a new dance, it's a whole new idea of what dance can be, which in many of these cases, like painters, has nothing even to do with theater . . . And then of course there was this unbelievable productivity—of course there were a lot of people involved, you know, as many as 40 people sometimes, of whom 20, 25, perhaps 30 were active as choreographers. And every one of those concerts, of which there were a whole lot, had something extraordinary happen. Obviously there were a lot of bombs, too, which there are in everything.'

After so much freedom, some of the creators then began to react towards austerity again, but of a new kind. Yvonne Rainer in a manifesto in the *Tulane Drama Review* in 1965 said 'no to spectacle no to virtuosity no to transformations and magic and make-believe no to the glamour and transcendancy of the star image . . . no to style no to camp no to moving or being moved'. In a programme note in 1968 she raged (her word) at the 'narcissism and disguised sexual exhibitionism of most dancing'. At the same time, 'I love the body—its actual weight, and unenhanced physicality.' In a developing series of works under the title *The Mind is a Muscle* she developed a language of complex movements involving different parts of the body working simultaneously, but all in an un-rhetorical way. The recitation of a pornographic poem at one point, like the showing of a blue movie during the similar *Rose Fractions,* made the dirty verse or film seem silly and the movement the more pure by contrast.

Another young woman (the latest generation of American dance revolutionaries is maintaining the traditional lead of women in this field) has developed a choreographic style even more austere. This is Twyla Tharp, whose pieces are intellectually contrived by considerations of space and time. She apparently prefers a non-theatrical place for performing, and has been known for instance to seat her audience in a square facing inwards, then dance round the outside of the square. (Curiously, even if you cannot see, it is possible to sense where they have reached.) Her pieces have starts and stops, repetitions and pauses. The supporting dancers are all women, preventing any possibility of unintended sexual significance being read into the dances. No story, no music, no continuity.

Of her *Group Activities* she wrote that it 'was to be like a dictionary: a set of facts bearing no relation to one another other than that which cannot be eliminated, namely order. There were to be hundreds of these facts or units, ranging in length from $\frac{1}{4}$ second to 45 seconds. A large part of the problem in the definition of the units was to keep them apart. As the devices which would keep the units apart—such as a time-out between two units—are limited in number, using more than one of these separating devices threw the dances into sets. Also, perhaps by nature, things tend to come together into series, categories and sets . . . As we had not anticipated this when we began, we have accepted it now as a lesson learned from the piece.' The movement was timed in half-seconds, and prepared with grids, plans and schedules to ensure absolute co-ordination or in other cases absolute differentiation or any stage in between. In performance the floor was squared off and divided by lines of tape and a time-keeper sat by to call the count at times. The concentration demanded from an audience as well as from the dancers is great, but tiny differentiations in such a context can become fascinating.

Not that Tharp is always so austere in her exploration of time and number. In *100s* for the New York Dance Festival in Central Park she produced a three-part dance, each part comprising the same hundred 10-second phrases; but first they were done successively by two performers; then shared out among five to be completed in a fifth of the time; and finally simultaneously, one each by a hundred performers. The intellectual rigour of this is no less, but the contrast easier to grasp.

Notable in a different way among the new generation is Meredith Monk, whose use of mixed media or pure movement reflects her wish not to be 'bound by any single style'. In one early solo, *Break*, she tried to produce a dance 'in which the movements broke apart, a dance which would be like shattered glass. All the movements were sharp. And I'd say things like "watch out"—loaded words, but I'd say them in a flat tone of voice. I did that because I wanted to take things out of their contexts and put them into new contexts.'

Later she wanted to move away from 'dancey' dances. 'It's not that I don't like "dancey" dances. But I think we ought to expand our ideas of what dance can be so we can find out more information about the nature of movement itself, just as experimental composers, by abandoning conventional ideas of pitch and harmony, are finding out things about the nature of sound.' In *Duet for Cat's Scream and Locomotive* she used soundwaves inaudible to the ear although she claims that the brain perceives them. In this, 'the movement was very minimal . . . I liked creating movement like this, rather than going zam-zam all day long. Indeed, there may be too much zam-zam bombarding us in daily life. Slow dances make people realize they have eyes to see with. Some people complain that they can't watch my slow dances; they used to complain that they couldn't watch my fast dances.'

In one of her dances, she incorporated 'a serious performance (no parody, no "camp") of Fokine's *Dying Swan*. I wanted this to have an appearance comparable to that of an old photograph in a collage. Soviet ballerinas, after they've done *The Dying Swan*, often come out and do it again as an encore—I think that's so groovy! They may not realize it, but that's real experimental dance. Their "dying" twice is like me taking familiar things and putting them into unexpected contexts.'

STARTING FROM SCRATCH

Although there had been dance companies in Holland before, the country had no continuing tradition of dance. In this respect the extremely experimental nature of the companies founded there during the 1950s contradicts a generalization I made earlier. This contradiction is mainly because of the influence at a vital moment of Martha Graham, who took her company there during a European tour, and partly because of the continuing influence of various Americans working there.

Jaap Flier, the present director of Netherlands Dance Theatre, says that when he and Rudi van Dantzig—now director of the National Ballet—as very young dancers saw the Graham company they were 'mad about what we saw. It seemed so new, such a different approach, and we immediately wanted to do choreography of our own. He started *Night Island* and I started a work based on Kafka's *The Trial.*' Van Dantzig also has said that he 'got an education for years in one afternoon, watching a demonstration class by Martha Graham and company'.

Van Dantzig was the first Dutch choreographer to win an international reputation, but for a long time his position was an anomalous one, as principal choreographer to the National Ballet which persisted nevertheless in giving prominence to invited guest choreographers and also maintained a startlingly large repertory of revivals, more than any other company in the world—and most of them badly danced. In time however it became clear that Van Dantzig's experimental works were the company's chief claim to prestige and eventually he took over the artistic direction.

The repertory remained a mixed one, with productions of the old classical ballets and modern classics by Balanchine on the one hand, and modern dance works including contributions by Kurt Jooss and Pearl Lang on the other. Curiously and, as far as I know, uniquely, the company lists certain principals specifically as modern dancers, including Toer van Schayk who is also a painter and designs most of Van Dantzig's ballets, collaborating closely with him in the detailed development of the original conception, even to the extent that Van Dantzig works out the movements on Van Schayk and himself before teaching them to the dancers.

Van Dantzig's biggest success (created for his own company and later revived in America for the Harkness Ballet) was *Monument for a Dead Boy*. Inspired by the death of a young poet, it began with the death of the central character and then went back to trace his birth, childhood and formative influences, including a tender but abortive relationship with a young girl, disgust at his parents' love-making and his own homosexual encounters, including initiation with a kind of mass rape by schoolfriends in the changing room. These elements made the work somewhat controversial, but Van Dantzig explained 'After all we live in times when people can be naked and as they are, and no longer have to hide what is really in them. It all makes life so much more worth living, and also more free for a creative artist. This goes through all the arts now—in painting, in music, in everything. It's the fabulous thing about today—this honesty. It's what the whole beat scene is about. All this isn't just a fashion, for it involves everyone's life, not just a passing thing.' He went on to add that he was not particularly interested by beat or jazz clubs 'but I get a good deal from films, particularly from Fellini whose *8½* made a great impression on me. Actually, *Monument for a Dead Boy* is built like a Fellini film.'

Against the powerful theatrical and emotional impact of *Monument* can be set another side of Van Dantzig's work exemplified by *Moments*, a completely plotless work set to music by Webern, the Six Bagatelles and Five Pieces for String Quartet: terse, fragmentary music matched by choreography of equal economy and precision. It is a sequence of episodes, some lasting only a few moments. In each, the main movement is concentrated on just two or three of the dancers, or sometimes only one. The total effect, in Van Schayk's minimal designs of a few lines of red or blue, is like looking at a series of non-representational but related pictures, except that the immediacy of the dancing and the extra dimension of the movement add complexity and richness.

Something of both *Monument* and *Movements* can be found in *Epitaph*, a strange, complex work full of images of death combined into a pattern that makes poetic rather than logical sense, and set to two pieces by Ligeti, one of which is defined by the composer as implying 'certain associations with the old Requiem sequence'.

Whereas Van Dantzig began under Graham's inspiration and is now influenced by films, Hans van Manen, for many years joint director of Netherlands Dance Theatre, started with a great admiration for the ballets of Balanchine, Robbins and Petit, and nowadays says 'if anything inspires me it is modern painters and sculptors, the way they work and the ideas they work on'.

Dance Theatre was founded by a small group of dancers, mostly from the larger Netherlands Ballet (which later became the National company), who wanted to be a contemporary company and do serious creative work. With them as artistic director in the formative years was an American teacher and choreographer Benjamin Harkarvy, who had the aim of creating 'an atmosphere which is conducive to creative work. There are sometimes people who have perhaps a potential for choreography who don't grow up in the right milieu and nothing comes of it.' Having started his career interested only in classical ballet, he had given ballet classes to established modern dancers who were attracted by his reputation for an analytical approach, and he told me that through them 'I began to see dancing as movement and not as technique. I began to understand that there is something that must be present in a good dancer whether he is ballet or modern: that it comes from within and that he dances with his whole being. I began to see that the important thing is the vocabulary of the dance, and that the dancer must be so well equipped that he can cope with the vocabulary of the various choreographers. With the meeting of the classical technique and the modern dance, the vocabulary of dance is fantastically rich today.'

From the beginning, Dance Theatre had regular classes in both techniques and invited choreographers of both schools. It also adopted the policy that any member of the company could try to make a ballet if he wished. About ten or more works were mounted each year, all by living choreographers, most of them created specially for the company, and mostly to modern music.

Harkarvy's view was that 'the nineteenth century was the age of the ballerina, but I think that dance has now reached a time when the choreographer has become recognized as the central figure in his art just as the composer is the central figure in music'. Harkarvy's own ballets have tended to be rather straightforward, although some developed a strange atmosphere, such as the version of Berio's *Visage* which he created, a characterization to match the electronically developed nonsense-speech of which the music consists.

A remarkably iconoclastic young choreographer was soon developed within the company however in the person of Hans van Manen. From the beginning he took the line that 'messages are for literature, and dance is not literature. My care is only for the movement which is to be seen. I want the public to make whatever interpretation it wants.' Often in his work he would set himself a particular technical problem as the basis of constructing a ballet: to have every movement mirrored by another, for instance, or to have the dancers enter and leave the stage at fixed time-intervals. Curiously, this approach produced drama, not formalism. In *Metaphors* the mirror-movements led to a two-girl duet, a two-man duet and a linked pas de quatre into which the audience could read its own implications—or could simply reflect on the way some combinations carried overtones while others did not; in other words, the work left a choice for the audience of an intellectual, an emotional or a purely aesthetic observation. One interpretation specifically excluded from the male duet however was that of a homosexual relationship; with one man partnering, supporting, even lifting the other to his shoulder like a ballerina, Van Manen had difficulty in ensuring this and eventually found that the only solution was for them not to look at each other.

Looking plays a key part also in the ballet he set to John Cage's *Solo for Voice 1*. Van Manen wanted to work with a singer and two dancers for the sake of the conflict that would arise between them on stage. 'I wanted the singer to be a part of the idea. I asked her to come closer to the dancers. I wanted her very close, so that it was as if she was telling them what to do, although in the music and the text there is nothing of this. The text has absolutely nothing to do with what you see. I wanted to have two people completely occupied with themselves, and that the singer should be as close to them as possible. It was there that the "story" started, and it appears now that she is watching the dancers but the dancers never watching her. You get the feeling that when she sings she is inventing what you are seeing.' The effect is of a strange mating ritual, with the dancers very intent and solemn, most of the time on the floor, dressed in white, and the singer, very tall, in black velvet dress with an elaborately piled head of blonde hair, towering above them like a goddess-figure, or sometimes crouching close over them: a curious but compelling piece of theatre, although derived entirely from the formal situation.

Van Manen explains that 'it is no longer choreographers who influence me but the art of sculpting, of painting—and more than that it is the art *behind* the work of these people. I cannot be inspired by a sculpture or painting that is finished. I can only be inspired by the ideas of the artists of today who create work that is of today. It is the form, the "why".'

In *Squares* he collaborated directly with one of the artists he admires, Bonies, who designed a movable setting which imposed square shapes upon the action. There was a dais in the centre of the stage which was lifted out on wires, and a metal framework lowered in to hang either above the dancers' heads, around their waists, or vertically behind them; this frame was lined with both neon and ultraviolet lighting tubes. The movements were mostly slow and gentle, and always circumscribed by the setting. The effect was remote, cool, like kinetic sculpture rather than ordinary dancing; Van Manen told me that ideally he would like to watch it from a distance in a huge arena. It was made to be danced to Satie's *Trois Gymnopédies*, first on piano and then in orchestrated form, but for copyright reasons an adaptation by the conductor Zoltan Szilassy was adopted. In any case the movement and music were coexistent, not organically connected; Van Manen says that 'I don't like to use music with a note for every step, because then you use the music under the ballet and I want to use it beside the ballet'.

Sometimes he uses no music. His *Essay in Silence* is perhaps the most successful example of this genre; in fact the silence is punctuated by footfalls, amplified heartbeats and other sounds. One trio is given a surprisingly tense sexual drama by having the men call out at the end of each phrase of movement, and having the girl at one point stand and laugh at them. The final sequence is accompanied by, but unrelated to, a passage of organ music.

In *Situation* the accompaniment is drawn from commercial recordings (of shots, engine noises, rainfall and other sounds) published for amateur film-makers. In this ballet Van Manen collaborated with another Dutch painter, Jean-Paul Vroom, who provided the specified situation, a room measuring $8 \times 6 \times 4$ metres (its proportions emphasized by having the walls lined with outsize graph paper), with a single door and a digital clock showing the actual time. Within this enclosed situation five couples acted out various sexual or personal relationships of aggression and violence; a woman dominating or dominated by a man, one man or woman tempting or taunting another. The combination of realism and fantasy in the design was matched by the contrast between the heated drama within each pair's episode and the stylized beginning and flip, off-beat comic ending in which one man, having driven his partner into a gibbering wreck, returned again and again with different comic walks to deflate the atmosphere and raise again the whole question of realism versus illusion.

Jean-Paul Vroom joined with Van Manen also in his share of the ballet *Mutations*, a joint venture with Glen Tetley, who was at the time co-director with Van Manen of the company. They took two scores by Stockhausen and to these developed themes of change: in space, in time, in appearance, in nature. Tetley set the stage action, beginning with a ritualistic sequence in which dancers (in white tights with rings worn inside to make them look like jointed crustacean armour) slowly occupied the stage from a ramp leading right through the audience. Then the first of Van Manen's film sequences showed a naked man dancing in slow motion. Alternate passages of stage and film choreography developed and extended this contrast until a final nude duet which came like a calm benediction after preceding violence. The nudity naturally attracted much comment and big audiences, but in its context seemed perfectly natural and was not in fact publicized by the company, who were at least as much concerned about the formal developments in the work: the abstract expression of a theme, the combination of media and the opening up of the dance area with a forestage and ramp.

Possibly the creators had been partly inspired in this work by the company's collaboration in a mixed-media event with the English sculptor Peter Dockley (discussed in another chapter). Certainly Jaap Flier, who soon afterwards took over the artistic direction of the company, was very excited by the possibilities. Himself a choreographer (notably of a work to György Ligeti's avant-garde *Nouvelles aventures*, in which the dancers are eventually overwhelmed by sacks, like the droppings of the gods, into which they mysteriously disappear), he said after *Mutations* that he was no longer happy with traditional theatres for the company's work.

It's that box, that proscenium arch that bothers me. I found in *Mutations* how beautiful it is when you use a stage that really goes out into the audience. We should never use a curtain any more, as it makes a barrier and also a mixture of styles. We should really start to use space . . . a figure is so much more beautiful when it is really related to space and not just seen from the front. It's not necessary to go all the way into the audience, but if you do away with the curtain the whole theatre opens up. I find the whole way of using the orchestra is of another age and not right for a contemporary company. If you don't use an orchestra then you have to approach things differently. By opening up the stage, doing away with curtains and orchestra, there is also a limitation but it immediately demands a new approach and a new style. I would like to do this, but it will take a long time before people will want to cope with this kind of situation.

ACROSS FRONTIERS—GLEN TETLEY

Glen Tetley, an American, is much less admired in America than in Europe. Americans will generally explain that this is because Europeans have seen too little modern dance and have less demanding standards. It might be however that Europeans are seeing something in Tetley's work which his compatriots have so far failed to recognize. This is the beginning of something which has already had much lip service: a new style combining elements of both ballet and modern dance.

Tetley himself says 'I am very moved by the brilliance, the lift, the drive, the lyricism of classical ballet. I am equally moved by the whole dark spectrum of Graham's theatre, world and tech- nique. Perhaps it's too wide an embrace, but I wanted actively to experience both of these worlds.' He took his first lesson at the Graham school and studied intensively with Hanya Holm, acting as her choreographic assistant as well as dancing in her company. Many (perhaps most) American modern dancers take ballet classes too, and Tetley went to Margaret Craske and Antony Tudor for these; but whereas generally they are done only as exercises, Tetley put his classical technique to use. He has been a leading dancer with both Graham and the classically based Ballet Theatre; he has mounted works for the British and Swedish Royal Ballets as well as for modern dance companies in Utah, Tel Aviv and many points in between. He says:

Or course there is a division, everything is twofold, there is heaven and hell, sea and shore, day and night. People will arbitrarily say there's classical and there's modern, but I don't believe it. There are two types of dancing—good and bad. There is that which I consider classic (and classic is a much misused term) which means that it is pure of its form, there is no other overtone existing at that time, and this doesn't only belong to classic ballet . . . A dancer will always keep his own natural quality; a soprano is a soprano, a tenor a tenor, a bass a bass, and with dancers there are those gifted in a more purely-centred, classical, Apollonian cool type of performance; then there are the Bacchic people who are meant to pull off centre.

Because of this view, strengthened during the times when he was associated, first as dancer and choreographer, later as joint director, with the similarly inclined Netherlands Dance Theatre, Tetley has developed his own approach calling on elements from both techniques. Norman Morrice, having seen Tetley create and revive several works for Ballet Rambert, considered that 'in his work you don't see where the seam is between classical and modern. He respects both techniques but only uses them to get the theatrical effect or the theatrical meaning that he requires.' He also commented on the effect of Tetley's working with dancers who had studied both techniques: 'He demands more and more because he knows that he can give a movement that one would say was modern (whatever that means), but unless a dancer had at one time learned to do, say, six decent classical pirouettes he would not be able to do this movement. This is the extension, though it isn't obvious unless you have studied both and seen how it is all progressing. But it is there, and it opens a whole new future.'

More important, though, than his eclectic technique and the greater freedom of expression this brings is the use to which Tetley puts this expression. When he turned to choreography, his work was from the first rich in complex multiple images, full of meanings and allusions, but emotionally and dramatically straightforward. *Pierrot Lunaire*, given on his first programme, is full of hidden depths, because in making it 'things floated to the surface—memories of situations in my life that I wanted to work into the fabric of the ballet'. The intellectual implications, too (the allusions for instance to elements of the ancient Roman theatre and the commedia dell'arte that grew from it; the cross references to *Petrushka*, which was written in the same year as Schoenberg's score; the alliance of Brighella and Columbine against Pierrot, and the latter's astonishing final gesture of acceptance and forgiveness) are enough to keep the spectator alert at repeated performances, quite apart from the strong impact of the characters, each capable of many interpretations. But the actual structure is straightforward, and the gesture is that of clear mime.

Gradually Tetley began to evolve a more allusive style. In *Freefall* 'I wanted to work without any scenario or preconceived direction. I wanted to achieve between people a freefall of associations and relationships . . . It is something I have wanted to do, but have always been terrified of being so unprepared and of working just at the moment . . . I have always had a theme or an image of who the people were, and where they stood in time or space. But now I wanted just to start on balance, then the fall, that moment of the jumper who leaves the plane. It is a kind of exhilaration to fall.' And so he created a work of no specific situation or narrative but of jagged nervous and sexual tensions, with a cast of two men and three women (ensuring one kind of imbalance from the start) thrown into every possible combination and conflict.

In *Ziggurat* the starting point was Assyrian remains in the British Museum and the idea of the ancient pyramidal stepped temples which Tetley equated also with the Tower of Babel and the Hanging Gardens of Babylon. Men run through the metal structures of Nadine Baylis's design; their god (a dominating figure made in their own image) topples and has to be supported and warmed in an attempt at sustenance; two men in turn dance violent duets with the god, and a third (on an unrolled strip of plastic material that might be the path to heaven) with an angel; at the end all the men, their earlier agitation calmed, bow deeply and the god, unexpectedly, rises among them. As direct narrative this is ludicrous; as a suggestive exploration of man's nature and his religious needs, and a parallel between ancient and modern life, it is gripping.

Other works have continued this double focus of time. *Arena* was inspired by a pre-Colomban ball court but the scene, with stackable metal chairs and a washbasin with running water, is also unmistakably modern. The action of *Field Figures* is probably meant to occur in the emotional lives of two people locked in an ecstatic sexual embrace, suspended in time rather than consecutive. *Circles* is related both to modern Olympics and to the Olympus of classic myth. Equally, all these works are capable of interpretation on different levels. In *Arena* for instance there is a conflict between one man of outstanding bearing and authoritative manner with a younger rival, and a novice for whose interest they are both concerned. It may be 'about' the casual, almost non-sexual homosexual relationships found in some sporting contexts, or the precarious situation of the leader or champion in any sphere, or even something as specific as Theseus with his bulldancers, since the music is Subotnik's *The Wild Bull* and the men have painted their bodies in the Cretan manner. The ambiguity is no weakness, rather an enrichment; as the different layers of possibility are seen they add to the different levels at which the work can be enjoyed. With a direct narrative this would be impossible, or possible only on the rather unsatisfactory level of an allegory. Tetley's kind of construction goes as far beyond allegory as a poetic metaphor does beyond a simple simile. Tetley says:

I don't look for ideas. Sometimes they suddenly happen, and that's marvellous. I have had certain things come together all of a sudden sparked by, say, a piece of music, something I have suddenly read, or a picture. But that is not the total thing, merely the spark that sets it off. Usually it is taking something which has stimulated me and bringing it close to personal experience. I work best on an emotional basis; I work least well when I start from exterior and work by design. I am, finally, not all that rational. I wish I could be, as I admire order, but for me it is very hard to exact order unless it grows from some kind of centre.

TRANSFORMATION SCENE

Sometimes it can be that not just an individual but a whole company will consciously aim at something entirely new and revolutionary. The most extreme example is that of Ballet Rambert, a long-established British company which in 1966 suddenly changed its whole style, policy, repertory and performing pattern.

Marie Rambert's original company had been, a generation earlier, a small group presenting mainly new works by new choreographers, with just a few revivals from the Diaghilev repertory or old Russian classics. Over the years economic circumstances had caused this to evolve gradually into a medium-sized company still trying to do modern works but compelled most of the time to tour with modest, stylish, imaginative but under-danced classic revivals. Frustrated at this, Rambert and her principal choreographer Norman Morrice decided to do away with the corps de ballet and revert to a small company entirely of soloists, producing as many new works as possible. At the same time they introduced Graham classes to supplement their daily classical ballet classes.

The first effect of this, said Morrice, 'seeing the two techniques being taught side by side, is that the newer one is making the dancers rediscover the one that has been a habit for so many years. They are finding excitement in the old technique just by virtue of the contrast with the new one.'

Originally the idea was to perform quite a few of the works which had been specially created for the old Rambert company, but most of these were soon dropped. Morrice said the trouble was that by comparison with the newer ballets 'the conventions are so very different—of lighting, of design, of costume, of music. To mix them doesn't seem to work.' In the case of Tudor's *Dark Elegies*, this was overcome by scrapping the old backcloths and relying on lighting effects to establish the mood and also the change near the end.

Rambert's experience underlines how much the new-wave ballets differ from traditional works, not only in choreography but in all their other constituent parts. Even before the deliberate change in the company's image, Morrice's own creations had begun to introduce experimental elements. Several of his early works were designed, for instance, by Ralph Koltai, one of the leaders in a new approach to design in the English theatre. His work and that of his colleagues and pupils for Rambert, for the National Theatre and for the Royal Shakespeare company, substituted constructed sets for painted backcloths, and costumes that were atmospherically or poetically apt rather than realistic.

From the beginning, Morrice's ballets concerned themselves with credible people in contemporary circumstances: two brothers in a poor neighbourhood fighting over a girl; the construction of a dam in the desert and the social and personal conflicts this brought. Morrice wanted his works to deal with serious topics: *The Travellers* used a plot about a ballet company stranded at a foreign airport to suggest a moral about how easily dictatorship could grow from petty restrictions to complete tyranny. It was only with the company's new policy however that he found the technical vocabulary to give his ideas full expression.

In this respect *Hazard*, his first creation after the change-over, marks a turning point. In technique and construction (even in the titles of the sections—'Daughters of Eve', 'Gymnasium of Adam') *Hazard* was strongly influenced by Martha Graham, whose company appeared in London shortly before its première. It seemed at first like a complete breakthrough from Morrice's earlier style but soon appeared as only a halfway mark. Further influenced by Glen Tetley and Anna Sokolow, both of whom staged works for Rambert, Morrice trimmed off a lot of superfluities and reworked one of the essential themes from *Hazard* (again, the relationships of two men, one woman) into abstract form in *1-2-3*, where the cutting away of literary complications, the almost sculptural quality of the groupings, coupled with a vigorously simple technique and very subtle relationship to the music resulted in a much finer work. Morrice summed up the moral; to concentrate on 'the actual form of the piece and not allow the ideas, if they are too prolific, to destroy the physical structure and drama'.

Emboldened by this, Morrice went on to develop his new style, notably in *Blindsight* with its images of physical and emotional blindness and cruelty implying a strong reaction against widespread thoughtless inhumanity of man to man. As joint director of the company, however, he attached even more importance to developing new creative talent among the dancers. Frequent new productions, some special workshop programmes in collaboration with the Central School of Art and Design and a children's programme conceived and produced by the dancers themselves, all gave opportunities to aspiring choreographers. Two in particular showed distinctive and innovating talents. John Chesworth started with *Time Base*: half poetic fantasy, half science fiction, dealing with different aspects of time: historical, scientific, emotional. One solo was set to a text adapted from the dictionary definitions of time; this was danced first by a man but the alternate cast was a woman—something perfectly natural in so sexless a context, but unlikely to be thought of in the ordinary way of things.

In *'H'* Chesworth showed white-coated assistants in a clean, antiseptic laboratory calmly recording the death-throes of grey, shrivelled, pitiful creatures whose state was contrasted with the neat, trim, tidy rows of sleek cylindrical bombs under dust covers waiting to provide a further group of victims. In *Pawn to King 5* he treated a theme of sudden and unprovoked violence and its repercussions, partly in mimed terms (a Kabuki ritual suicide) but largely in abstract dance images, leading on to an entirely danced work *Four According* based on the real and fictional selves of Scott and Zelda Fitzgerald.

Whereas Chesworth started with theatrical ideas and later developed a choreographic expression, Christopher Bruce began with a light dance work, *George Frideric*, to Handel music 'mainly as an exercise in putting a ballet together' and then went on to 'try and combine drama with movement' and to 'get down to saying things that were inside me' in *Living Space*. For this duet about the beginnings, rise and decline of a love affair he first thought of working to silence but 'I ended up by using just words, prose written by a young poet . . . the words stand on their own. When you are watching it is difficult sometimes to hear what is being said because you are concentrating on the movement; but it doesn't really matter if you cannot hear the words too well because they act as a kind of music through the piece.'

Bruce's aim in *Living Space* was 'to do things that were closer to me, more personal' and the effect is almost embarrassingly intimate to watch in its expression of real feelings. He says that 'Movement is so emotional, possibly more emotional than straight theatre or films, anyway it is for me'. Having worked with words and movement, he is keen that dance should continue to move into many different areas: 'There are really no limits, I hate to limit any form of art, there should be no boundaries. It is exciting to move in all different kinds of direction; even if it ends in failure, at least we shall have learned something . . . What is ballet? It's dance on the stage. If it's something like, say, Chesworth's *"H"* with things moving on the stage, even if they are crawling about, grovelling, clawing at their faces, they are moving, they are expressing something, there's emotion there. It's still movement, and dance covers an immense range of movement—all movement from blowing your nose to doing a double tour en l'air.'

FROM SCULPTURE TO DANCE

When a sculptor turns to involving his work with dance, three possibilities arise. He can make simply an environment for the dancers and choreographer to work in, as Isamu Noguchi has consistently and successfully done for Graham, Cunningham and others, or as when a sculpture by Martha Pan provided the context and impetus for Maurice Béjart's *Le Teck*. Secondly, he can bring movement into his sculpture, either with a straightforward piece of kinetic art, or with a moving structure which has so many planned variables that it actually gives an illusion of dancing; this is what the young British artist Peter Logan has done with his Mechanical Ballet, in which he has even on one occasion (for Scottish Theatre Ballet's experimental evening of *Ploys*) added live dancers.

The third course is that taken by a contemporary of Logan,

Peter Dockley, who says that 'I moved away from sculpture because it didn't enable me to explore as many ideas as I wanted to. I think this is becoming a common situation with artists everywhere and in all branches. The result of this is that all barriers between media are breaking down, and these media are often coming together under the general heading of theatre.' Dockley first staged a series of events in a (literally and metaphorically) underground club called The Middle Earth, then turned to using sculptural ideas in a context involving also dancers and others. He has however avoided the conventional theatre situation for his work; when invited to submit ideas for a ballet to be presented at Sadler's Wells by Netherlands Dance Theatre, his first response was 'Have you twelve dancers willing to work completely submerged?' Unfortunately nothing came of this attempt to revive the theatre's past aquatic glories.

Partly this aversion from a conventional stage comes from his sculptural bias, being used to three physical dimensions as against the flat surface of painting, but he says also that he has been influenced by the work of John Cage, Ann Halprin, Robert Morris and others on alternatives to the traditional theatre situation, also by 'my own observations of forms such as a cricket field, a football game, a golf match, a religious meeting, law courts. All these forms have their own shape, logicality and their own characteristics. Compare the stage situation—the audience set out in tight rows in the auditorium looking in one direction, one focal point—with an athletics match with runners on the outside encircling the field, then in the centre a whole series of activities such as javelin throwing, long jump, high jump and so on. This contains a whole series of stimulants, points of focus, and this could provide an interesting point of departure for performance.'

One of Dockley's early experiments with dancers was an event called *4 Sounds 4 Structures* in which four differently shaped structures of tubular metal were set up in the four quarters of a large hall. A dancer occupied each of these and there was a musician in each corner of the hall. The audience was free to move around or between the structures. The aim was 'to make the audience more aware of space. I hoped that after a while they would be able to contemplate space and separate activities in space.' Each dancer was asked not to try to express anything on an emotional level, simply to demonstrate the characteristics of the allotted structure; for instance, one 'involved very strong lines and four suggested planes, these in turn suggesting linear extensions into space. The dancer here was asked to move along the strongest lines the structure afforded, asked to complement the plane shapes in her body.'

The separate activities within each structure were entirely unco-ordinated and the dancers were still developing movement during the performance, on the principle that 'the audience is very much aware of something which is set, finished, and from which

K

they are creatively excluded'. The musicians, using voices, bowed cymbal, gongs and prepared piano, were asked to improvise a line of sound passing round the edges of the hall from one to another, thus further defining space.

Dockley suggests that in the past:

the audience have passively received finished ideas. What these new forms are embodying is a new audience-performance relationship both in physical terms and in intellectual terms. Before, an audience was almost excluded in the creative process; now an audience is being invited to contribute to the flow of creativity. If, for instance, elements are put in front of them that are unrelated, then it is up to the audience to bring them into some sort of relationship if they so wish. In John Cage's term, 'appealing to an audience's structuring facility'. I think a distinction has to be made between the various types of participation. A number of things are happening at the moment which deal with physical participation—full stop! But that in itself is a limited situation. What I tried to do was to involve the audience physically in space.

Dockley's later development of this kind of activity progressed in two ways. One was an elaboration of a similar situation, involving also acrobats and gymnasts, kendo fighters, some elaborate 'event costumes' suggesting spacemen, vapours, fireworks and smoke bombs let off by men wearing clothes made of pieces of glittering mirror or sludgy red rubber.

The other development arose from a commission to create a work for Netherlands Dance Theatre. His first idea was to block off the stage with a ramp descending at a 30° angle from the back wall to the feet of the front row of the audience; this proved impracticable so instead they moved into an open-plan theatre in The Hague called The Hot. This is usually set up with playing space in the middle and audience on three sides, but instead the audience were moved to the middle with slopes all round them and a net overhead, with figures moving across this and one permanently suspended there. The dancers were put in elaborate costumes dictating special ways of moving, and light was used to focus attention different ways at different times. At one point there was a confetti storm, dry-ice smoke dripping from white balloons and figures moving about within this like a confused mass, a layer of white above the audience which later clarified into perspective again.

Whatever its possible effect on Dockley's own future work, this production, called *Never Never Land*, had an important influence on the general trend of Netherlands Dance Theatre's policy and went a long way towards its creator's ambition of evolving a performance that will 'work both as a spectacle and an environment' and to bring about a fusion of 'audience and performance,

environment and spectacle, inside and outside through the flow of
ideas, energy and states'.

OUTPOSTS

You can see how circumstances affect experiment by watching
what happens when ideas are transported from one spot to
another. Take the situation in eastern Europe where all ballet is
inevitably influenced by Soviet styles and ideas. Both Hungary
and Czechoslovakia have sent small experimental companies on
tour. Both appeared to have been influenced by films of Béjart,
but the ideas they had taken had been transmuted into their own
idiom. The Sopiane Ballet from Pecs tended to a rather solemn
manner, too consciously concentrating on the plot rather than
other ingredients. The Studio Ballet of Prague had the advantage
of that city's lively theatrical tradition; they too gave the impression that a well-intentioned theme was taken at face value
irrespective of how conveyed, but their repertory was enlivened
by some more entertaining pieces, not least a version of Bartók's
Miraculous Mandarin which, by stripping away inessentials,
allowed the dance characterization to make its point. Both Sopiane
and the Studio Ballet did versions of a work *Hiroshima*: admirably
intentioned in its wish to make dance provide a social comment, but
in fact depending entirely on programme notes, since the character
supposed to represent Conscience was merely an attractive young
woman in tights who could as easily have stood for Libido or
almost any other quality. This taking the intention for the deed is
not an exclusively East-European attribute; it applied equally for
instance to Joseph Lazzini's $E = Mc^2$ for the Marseille Ballet—
meant as an attack on the atomic bomb, but looking more like a
Folies Bergère number with the spirit of the bomb as a beauty
queen (Miss Nuclear Fission?).

Exactly the opposite of these various works in style and approach is Oscar Araiz's *Symphonia*, one of the most substantial
works in the repertory of the San Martin Ballet which he directs in
Buenos Aires. This clearly owes a lot to ideas similar to those of
many different choreographers (Nikolais, Robbins, Tetley, Van
Manen) but possibly derived by hearsay rather than direct influence. The themes of birth and death, fear and courage, challenge,
discovery, love and sex, opposition and ambition, are not stated
but suggested in an abstract form. A world in which everyone is
alone even when with others is implied for instance by the opening
Perceptions in which the dancers make individual entries in
opposition to each other, and a girl's attempts to pick up an object
centre-stage are interrupted fearfully by the appearance of a man
on the other side. A collage score by a series of modern composers
makes a powerful effect as accompaniment.

Araiz is trying to implant new ideas in a country hitherto used mainly to classical ballet, although lively enough in the other arts. In Sweden, Birgit Cullberg is concerned to fan fresh life into an existing willingness to experiment. Quite apart from living memories of the highly original Ballets Suédois, even the Royal Ballet at the Stockholm Opera House mixes Limón and Robbins, Tetley and Tudor with its *Swan Lake* and *Romeo and Juliet*. So at the Dramatic Theatre round the corner, the Cullberg Ballet can easily afford to do its own *Romeo and Juliet* to a digest version of the Prokofiev score, dance Cunningham's *Summerspace* and Jooss's *Green Table* and to present a version of the Orpheus legend, *Eurydice is Dead*, in terms inspired by the artist Palle Nielsen. This shows an unmistakably contemporary world, entirely in black and white, with the projected designs of Orjan Wiklund literally a moving picture: a film that pans across an urban landscape, great squares shut in by vast buildings, with wires overhead to give a caged feeling. Sometimes it zooms in to give a close-up effect, then draws away again to reveal that the surroundings have mysteriously changed. Seen in front of this frighteningly inconstant scenery, the dancers look like people from a new-wave French movie, with Eurydice abducted by the secret police and Orpheus climbing vainly across precipitate heights to reach her. The ingredients are more production than choreography, but mixed in a way that works.

Even in a town like London with a great deal of dance activity it is still possible to have set down a little outpost of an imported style. This is exactly what has happened with the London Contemporary Dance Theatre, based on a school founded by Robin Howard 'not to try and transplant American modern dance to this country; it is to try and develop a native style appropriate to the bodies and outlook of British people, to our climate and the rest of our culture. We have chosen to base it upon the Graham approach and technique because we feel that this is far more developed than any alternative.'

Robert Cohan, one of Graham's partners who became director of the London company, said, 'I don't find the physiques here particularly different . . . but the temperament certainly is. One of the problems has been to make people come out more . . . to expand as human beings and to expand in terms of dance which they are not used to doing. They are used to holding everything in.' Perhaps because of this, among the many members of the company and visiting choreographers who created works for the organization in its early days, the most successful included two American dancers, Noemi Lapzeson and Robert North, who made small humorous and dramatic pieces involving speech as well as dance. Also a young English dancer, Richard Alston, whose works were based on the quiet development of a small range of movement in abstract patterns. An important influence on him was the Dutch dancer-choreographer Pauline de Groot, herself a student of Cunningham and of Erick Hawkins, a former Graham principal who had gone his own way, including a study of American Indian dancing with its percussive accompaniment and its ritualistic use of non-narrative movement, elements taken up successfully by both de Groot and Alston.

With its base at The Place, used also by many unusual dance and theatre companies visiting London, the London Contemporary Dance Theatre is in a position to be expecially susceptible to international influences, yet the strong Graham basis of the training has meant that most of the early works created for it have been dutiful copies of her technique without her enlivening spirit.

The use of The Place also as headquarters of the musical ensembles (first the Pierrot Players, later Fires of London) run by the composer Peter Maxwell Davies brought about several collaborations, including the most notable of all works yet to spring from the organization, *Vesalii Icones*, a composition 'for cello solo, small instrumental group, and dancer' created by Maxwell Davies in collaboration with the dancer William Louther.

The idea of this came originally from the anatomical drawings of the sixteenth-century physician Andreas Vesalius; in fourteen illustrations he strips down the human body from its fleshy state to a skeleton. On these fourteen images the composer superimposed the idea of the Stations of the Cross. Musically and choreographically there are also superimpositions: 'in the music, there are three levels—plainsong, "popular" music and my own music derived from the other two' while the dancer has 'a parallel set of superimpositions—(1) the Vesalius illustrations, (2) the Stations of the Cross, and (3) his own body'. Each dance 'starts with the body position of the Vesalius illustration . . . then moves to express the parallel "Stations" situation, but the dance is not an attempt to act out the Vesalius drawing or the "Station"—it is an abstract from both.' The collaboration between dancer and composer extends even to including the former at one point as a musician, in the Mocking of Christ where he 'plays, on an out of tune piano, a garbled Victorian hymn (a musical style which I consider almost the ultimate musical blasphemy) and subsequently turns this into a cheery foxtrot'. Intellectually this structure would clearly make for a formidable work; by enabling Louther, in only his second attempt at choreography, to create a marvellously composed and sustained solo for himself lasting some forty minutes (longer than most complete ballets), and by the emotional impact which his dancing in turn lent to some not easily accessible music, the whole enterprise suggested the possibility of much mutual enrichment of music and dance if a collaboration on this level could be repeated.

Conclusion and prospect

If one thing is clear about the experiments being made in dance all over the world today, it is that nothing is clear. Every theory held by any practitioner is contradicted by another; every attempt towards one objective is matched by another in the opposite direction. The only view held in common by every serious creative artist is that change of some sort is necessary; nobody is content to leave things as he finds them unless his talent is so small and imitative as to be negligible.

The most obvious differentiation and the easiest to define, but in my view by no means the most important, is in respect of technique. For something like half a century now, modern dance in one form or another has stood as a completely self-sufficient rival to the traditional classical ballet technique. The likelihood that either will completely defeat the other is remote. With many of the best young American, British and Russian choreographers firmly committed to preserving its purity and extending its expressiveness, classicism is not going to die out in the immediate future. Nor, having spread so widely in so short a time, is modern dance going to wither away.

What may well disappear, however, is the clear barrier between the two techniques. It is not so far back that supporters of either one were likely to be opponents of the other; their practitioners and audiences were mutually exclusive. Hanya Holm was the first person I heard suggest that the only valid distinction between dancers was whether they were good or bad; that was about twenty years ago and she put it forward as an unusual view. Now it is widely accepted. On a recent journey, for example, I happened to meet Merce Cunningham and Margot Fonteyn in different towns; almost the first words of each were to ask after the other, and Fonteyn discussed also the project urged by some friends for the two of them to dance together.

Some elements from each form have already entered the other. The advantages of this are expressed by Glen Tetley, one of the growing number of dancers and choreographers with experience of both:

If the art we are involved in is of any use it is in a state of flux, it's growing. The roots we hang on to, but that which we are working on from day to day has to be growing from all the influences around it, and if it is not, then it is dead. Classical ballet has changed in a marvellous way and it is going to change even more; contemporary dance has changed and is not what I started with twenty years ago but is going into a whole new period away from emotional power and into a period of form and the enjoyment of form for form's sake, of relaxation and technical prowess and all those things that formerly were only the province of classical ballet.

As each form incorporates some elements of the other, the gap between them grows less and the possibility of an eventual amalgamation greater. The vocabulary of movement available for a choreographer to choose from becomes richer with this increased choice.

It is not only in respect of technique that the appearance of dance works has been changing and will surely continue to change. Ponderously designed works have continued side by side with those adopting a new simplicity, realistic painted sets are used as well as three-dimensional ones, but there is no doubt which is more in accord with the spirit of the times. More important than any question of taste or fashion is the stimulus given to choreographers in many instances by a setting which provides an environment within which the dancers move, rather than merely a background; producers have found that exactly the same thing applies to plays. It is to some extent new and revolutionary, but in its basic attitude it is a reversion to the attitudes which served the theatre for many centuries before a more pompous and sentimental style grew up in comparatively recent times, and this encourages me to think that it will last.

Music too is going to continue to force and encourage dance into new experiments. Most people still prefer listening to music in older styles, but most composers prefer to write in new styles, so inevitably the amount of modern music will increase at the same time as new audiences grow up who accept it more easily because they have been used to it all their lives. If the composer offers the choreographer a work based on the sounds of actual life, or minute intervals of tone, or speech-sounds recorded and adapted, or any of the other possibilities now open to him, the choreographer is able to set to that music whatever kind of movement he thinks appropriate; but the content and purpose of the movement had better be equally attuned to the contemporary world, or it is going to look silly. The motto must be John Cage's: 'We're passing through time and space. Our ears are in excellent condition.'

Whatever kind of music he chooses, the choreographer's options as to the rhythmic and emotional relationship of his movement with that music are now wide open. From Lopukhov's belief that he must follow it exactly, to Nikolais's use of it simply as an accompaniment, anything goes. Yet from Nijinsky to Van Manen, and above all in the dominating team of Cage and Cunningham, the belief has been growing that the most satisfactory relationship is coexistence rather than dependence. Since the freedom which this gives to choreography is wished also by those who manage without any music at all, it is going to remain the choice of at least a substantial minority of choreographers. Yet the wish of a composer like Zimmermann to develop the interaction of music and dance, the avidity with which Balanchine seized on almost any scrap of new composition by Stravinsky and transmuted it into dancing, the example of mutual gain afforded in the composition and choreography of *Vesalii Icones*—all these suggest that other lines of approach are going to remain open.

A few years ago, it would have seemed inevitable that music, dance, speech and acting were going to combine in a new medium known as total theatre. That idea, in the way it was understood then, is probably completely dead; what people imagined was some kind of super-intelligent musical, with each of the ingredients in its own little package, but neatly shaped together so that they all fitted in. In practice the aims of those who wanted total theatre have been realized but in a different, far more casual form. Choreographers have no hesitation now in mixing speech, song or films into their works if they think it will help. Playwrights, opera composers and their producers, feel a similar freedom. In addition there has grown up a new generation of people, not strictly identifiable as falling into any one of these categories (although they will generally tend in the direction of one or another), who present either on stage, or in other surroundings, prepared activities involving various media. These may be as simple as the group in New York who take off their clothes, dance in the street and are away again before the police arrive. They may on the other hand be as elaborate as any formal theatrical show. They may use dancers as an element in what is primarily a work of visual art, or may aim towards an effect of dancing without dancers. Either way they will, as examples have already shown, exert an influence on more orthodox dance presentations.

Film is the outside medium which has already had the biggest impact on many young choreographers; many say that they have modelled their structure on that of the cinema, and Béjart goes so far as to say that 'for ten years, even more, for fifteen or twenty years, the two arts from which I have learned anything are music and the cinema . . . above all the cinema, it is the only place where one learns anything about our time'. Whether this process can extend much further, except in regard to the development of individual creative artists, is problematical. Thanks to the influence of films, ballet has already broken away from its old need for a straightforward structure like an old-fashioned play, and has found the possibilities of flashback, simultaneity, a completely free fantasy or whatever other shape is appropriate to a given work. Possibly there might be more use of film as part of the stage action, either to relate the people and happenings on stage to actual historical events (as MacMillan did in *Anastasia*), or to make possible contrasts in manner and timing, such as Van Manen showed in *Mutations*, especially in the sequences which involved drastically slowing down the movement to make actions performed in a few seconds last for several minutes.

In its themes, dance has now claimed and won for itself a choice as free and wide-ranging as it has in respect of music. It is impossible to generalize when different innovators have been equally and simultaneously concerned to establish serious themes for dance and to rid it of any themes at all. Yet on the whole it is safe to say that nowadays, if a ballet is to have a theme at all, that theme will generally be expected to bear some relationship to contemporary life or interests; the days when fairy-tales or simple myths were thought obviously suitable ballet stories are past. A new, allusive way of conveying themes has also been accepted, with the dance image interpreted directly instead of having to be converted first into literary terms. Often nowadays to try to explain a dance work in words simply robs it of much of its meaning, which is much clearer in movement than in any other terms. This is as it should be. A great many choreographers are happy, too, that the interpretation of their work should remain with the audience, and it is interesting that this applies to Béjart, whose works have a definite non-choreographic purpose and content, as well as to Cunningham who is concerned primarily with movement and its relationship to time.

In regard to content, three views are possible. On the one hand, the wish expressed by Nikolais and by many of the youngest modern dance creators for 'motion, not emotion'. On the other, the wish of classical choreographers like Tudor, MacMillan and Darrell for people to be moved by what they see. Perhaps on each side there has been a valuable tendency to stress those qualities which their own branch of the art of dance has lacked in the past. In between these extremes stands the belief of Robbins and others (and I suspect this may represent the opinion of most creators who have moved from one branch of their profession to another) that the motion makes the emotion: a view which explains and justifies a wider range of works than either of the other possible opinions—which is not to say that these also are not both tenable and often beneficial.

One thing that applies equally to these various lines of approach is that the surface of the finished work, the whole look of the thing, is at the moment likely to be a lot more tranquil, more 'cool' than would have been the case a few years ago. Whether this is just a swing of the pendulum, to be as quickly reversed, is difficult to say; but I suspect it is partly connected with a general new attitude to dance and will therefore remain as a continuing influence. The justification for this thought is that dance has become accepted as a serious art form, not just a light entertainment to pass the time. Also, although stars and star performances remain, the work itself is now regarded more highly; so what people want to see is no longer the raw temperament of the performer but the finished object which he presents, the more clearly the better. It is the difference between the old-fashioned virtuoso concert, where the performer is all, the programme nothing, and the modern symphony concert, where a high degree of performing skill is expected and appreciated but the works are given their proper prominence.

There remains scope for the improvisatory approach too, but probably more on the fringes of dancing than in the mainstream. The Dancers' Workshop of Ann Halprin in California is largely concerned with making non-dancers able to involve themselves in

movement. The Stage Two experiments of James Roose Evans at
the Hampstead Theatre Club in London, although using dance
elements, are intended to produce a new kind of theatre rather
than a new kind of dance.

Not to be confused with improvisation is the conscious use of
chance techniques. John Herbert McDowell described how he made
an 18-note row for a musical composition simply from the first
notes of all the Bach gigues he happened to have in the house:
'And it was astonishing. It was very peculiar and something I
would never have done in my life. Now, the greatest thing about
chance is that you have to step in at a certain point and assert
an artistic prerogative. Chance is a great setter-offer of ideas, it's a
marvelous way of getting material, and peculiar material that
forces you into something different. And then at a certain point you
have to take control and shape it in a certain way.' Carolyn
Brown pointed out that 'the ways chance procedures are employed
are still only as interesting, as lively as the imagination of the
choreographer or composer' and that 'the works more often than
not bear the stamp of the person who made it, chance procedures
or not'. She also defined the purpose of using chance: 'If the
artist's impulse is to search for truth, then he was not coming close,
he felt, by concerning himself only with the known. And so these
particular artists, dissatisfied with the past as they'd come to
learn of it and with the present as it manifested itself in their
limited view of the world, chose to open themselves and their
work to the possible influences beyond their conscious knowledge.'
Or as Cage said, 'the field of awareness that's now open to us is
so big that if we're not careful we'll just go to certain points in it,
points with which we're already familiar. By using chance operations, we can get to points with which we are unfamiliar.'

The use of chance by Cunningham and Cage has proved so
enriching to their work that it is a wonder so few others have
followed them so far. Cage defined the novelty of their work as
derived 'from our having moved away from simply private human
concerns towards the world of nature and society of which all of
us are a part. Our intention is to affirm this life, not to bring order
out of chaos nor to suggest improvements in creation, but simply
to wake up to the very life we're living, which is so excellent once
one gets one's mind and one's desires out of its way and lets it
act of its own accord.' This is one respect in which the scope for
future experiment in dance is at least as great as anything yet
achieved, so that if others have the courage (and the stamina) to
follow where these pioneers have led, dance could be more transformed in the next quarter- or half-century than in the last.

Another field waiting to be opened up is that of consciously
training choreographers. Classical ballet companies have constantly complained that the number of good choreographers
arising at any one time is tiny. Modern dance has never found this
lack, and whenever people have set out deliberately to try to

develop new choreographers by adopting a more creative policy, talent has appeared. Having had some experience of this, Benjamin Harkarvy told me:

I don't think you can give a dancer talent; I don't think you can give a choreographic talent; but you can teach them an awful lot. There are sometimes people who have perhaps a potential for choreography who don't grow up in the right milieu and nothing comes of it. The cultivation of the choreographer and the cultivation of the dancer are to a certain point the same. I would love to see dancers trained like composers are trained, and musicians.

Besides this, there are two other possibilities which have scarcely begun to be employed yet. One is the immense scope available through systems of notating dances. It is only necessary to think how much music developed once a proper system of notation was available to see the possibilities for dance. I have heard of only one ballet actually composed entirely in notation and then taught to the dancers; so far dance notation has been only a means of recording dances once invented in the rehearsal hall. Yet there ought to be scope for an immensely richer orchestration of movement, for more subtle counterpoint and ingenious development than can be achieved by trial and error. At a guess, it seems likely that by the end of this century either notation will be in reasonably wide use for composition of dances, or, if it has been tried and proved deficient, that people will be trying to devise a new, improved notation which can serve that purpose.

The other possibility awaiting exploration is that of taking dance outside a conventional theatre setting. Béjart has used vast arenas (sports palaces and circus rings) for specially prepared works. Open stages, thrust stages, theatres in the round and various informal settings have been used from time to time, mainly by small organizations forced to appear where they can. Netherlands Dance Theatre have begun to explore the possibilities of reshaping the stage to bring dancers into a different involvement with their audiences. These and other possibilities will certainly be followed up, sometimes from choice, sometimes from necessity, and one consequence will be a change in the audience, with people brought in who are afraid or reluctant to patronize dance in its more formal establishments. This in turn will affect the kind of work given.

That much can be predicted. But the most interesting developments in the future, as in the past, will be those which cannot be predicted. Let Cage have the last word:

What is the nature of an experimental action? It is simply an action the outcome of which is not foreseen.

Sources of quotations

All previously published material is copyright by the original publishers and reprinted by kind permission of the copyright owners.

Opposite Introduction
MERCE CUNNINGHAM—*Changes: Notes on Choreography* (Frances Starr ed.) Something Else Press, New York 1968
MARTHA GRAHAM—quoted in *Martha Graham* (Karl Leabo ed.) Theatre Art Books, New York 1961
JOHN CAGE—*Silence* Wesleyan University Press, Connecticut 1961

Part I

The predecessors
RUTH ST DENIS—*The Legacy of Isadora Duncan and Ruth St Denis* (Walter Terry ed.) Dance Perspectives, New York 1960
HELEN TAMIRIS—ibid.
MARTHA GRAHAM—interview in *Dance and Dancers*, London February 1963
FRANCIS PICABIA—backcloth for scene 2 of *Relâche*; and manifesto published in *La Danse*, Paris November–December 1924

Where and when
CLIVE BARNES—review in *Dance and Dancers* March 1966
JILL JOHNSTON—article in *The Village Voice*, New York 21 January 1965; also reprinted in *Ballet Review* vol. 1 no. 6, New York 1967
JUDITH DUNN—'My Work and Judson's' and 'Judson: A Discussion' both in *Ballet Review* vol. 1 no. 6 1967

The new music for dance
HUMPHREY SEARLE—*Ballet Music—an Introduction* Cassell, London 1958
KARLHEINZ STOCKHAUSEN—*Kontakte* Deutsche Grammophon, Hamburg
BERND ALOIS ZIMMERMANN—'On the future of the ballet' in *International Ballet on German Stages* Prestel, Munich 1968
JOHN CAGE—*Silence*

About form and content
CYRIL BEAUMONT—preface to *The Complete Book of Ballets* Putnam, London 1937
GEORGE BALANCHINE—*Balanchine's New Complete Stories of the Great Ballets* (Francis Mason ed.) Doubleday, New York 1968
JOHN CAGE—*Silence*
MARTHA GRAHAM—interview in *Dance and Dancers* February 1963
MANFRED GRÄTER—interview with Horst Koegler in *Dance and Dancers* June 1970

The outsiders
GEOFF MOORE—interview in *Dance and Dancers* July 1969
DON MCDONAGH—review in *Dance and Dancers* November 1967

Part 2

Aspiring to the state of music—from Fyodor Lopukhov to George Balanchine

FYODOR LOPUKHOV—'Puti letmeistera' (Paths of the ballet master) Petropolis, Berlin 1925; translated from the Russian by Natalia Roslavleva in *Era of the Russian Ballet* Gollancz, London 1966

GEORGE BALANCHINE—*Balanchine's New Complete Stories of the Great Ballets*

Martha Graham and her contemporaries

MARTHA GRAHAM—Don McDonagh 'A Chat with Martha Graham' in *Ballet Review* vol. 2 no. 4 1968

DORIS HUMPHREY—letter to Clive Barnes published in *Dance and Dancers* March 1959

ANNA SOKOLOW—interview in *Dance and Dancers* July 1967

Man of all worlds—Jerome Robbins

JEROME ROBBINS—interview with Peter Brinson in *Dance and Dancers* November 1959; and a conversation with Edwin Denby in *Dance Magazine* July 1969

A chance for dance—John Cage and Merce Cunningham

MERCE CUNNINGHAM—*Changes*; and interview in *Ballet Review* vol. 1 no. 4 1966

JOHN CAGE—*Variations IV* (recorded live at the Fiegen/Palmer Gallery) Everest Records, Los Angeles 1968

CAROLYN BROWN—'On Chance' in *Ballet Review* vol. 2 no. 2 1968

Landscape with figures

FREDERICK ASHTON—'Au Revoir? A talk with Don McDonagh' in *Ballet Review* vol. 3 no. 4 1970

KENNETH MACMILLAN—'Structure and Dance' interview with Alexander Bland in *International Ballet on German Stages*

JOHN CRANKO—'Movements and Music' interview with Wilhelm Kill-mayer in *International Ballet on German Stages*

PETER DARRELL—unpublished interviews with Annette Massie, Josephine Falk and the author

Theatre of magic—Alwin Nikolais

ALWIN NIKOLAIS—interview in *Dance and Dancers* August 1969; 'The Omniloquence of Alwin Nikolais' in *Dance Magazine* April 1968; and the souvenir book of his 1969 tour

Twentieth-century package—France and Belgium

MAURICE BÉJART—Roger Stengele *A la recherche de Béjart* Théâtre Royal de la Monnaie, Brussels 1968

A zest for dance—Paul Taylor

PAUL TAYLOR—'Down with Choreography' in *Dance Magazine* February 1966, republished in *The Modern Dance* (Selma Jeanne Cohen ed.) Wesleyan University Press, Connecticut 1966; interview with Arthur Todd in *Dance and Dancers* November 1964; programme books of European tours; and conversations with the author

From both sides—Russia and the USA: recent developments

YURI GRIGOROVICH—interview in *Dance and Dancers* September 1966
ELIOT FELD—interview in *Dance and Dancers* January 1969
ROBERT JOFFREY—Clive Barnes 'Joffrey' in *Dance and Dancers* February 1967

Outside in

JOHN HERBERT MCDOWELL—'Judson: a discussion' in *Ballet Review* vol. 1 no. 6 1967
JAMES WARING—'Judson: a discussion' ibid.

Judson and after

JUDITH DUNN—'Judson: a discussion' ibid.; and 'My Work and Judson's' in *Ballet Review* vol. 1. no. 6 1967
YVONNE RAINER—commentary or spoken accompaniment at performances, recorded in *Dance and Dancers* November 1965; *Tulane Drama Review* 1965; and Jack Anderson 'Yvonne Rainer; The Puritan as Hedonist' in *Ballet Review* vol. 2 no. 5 1969
TWYLA THARP—'Group Activities' in *Ballet Review* vol. 2 no. 5 1969
MEREDITH MONK—'Comments of a Young Choreographer' in *Dance Magazine* June 1968

Starting from scratch

JAAP FLIER—interview in *Dance and Dancers* January 1971
RUDI VAN DANTZIG—interview in *Dance and Dancers* May 1966
HANS VAN MANEN—interviews in *Dance and Dancers* May 1967 and June 1969
BENJAMIN HARKARVY—unpublished interview with the author

Across frontiers—Glen Tetley

GLEN TETLEY—interview in *Dance and Dancers* December 1967
NORMAN MORRICE—interview in *Dance and Dancers* August 1968

Transformation scene

NORMAN MORRICE—interview in *Dance and Dancers* August 1968
CHRISTOPHER BRUCE—interview in *Dance and Dancers* September 1969

From sculpture to dance

PETER DOCKLEY—interviews in *Dance and Dancers* July 1968 and March 1969

Outposts

ROBIN HOWARD—interview in *Dance and Dancers* October 1966
ROBERT COHAN—interview in *Dance and Dancers* September 1967
PETER MAXWELL DAVIES—programme note of the Pierrot Players, Queen Elizabeth Hall, London 9 December 1969

Conclusion and prospect

GLEN TETLEY—interview in *Dance and Dancers* December 1967
JOHN CAGE—*Silence*
JOHN HERBERT MCDOWELL—'Judson: a Discussion' in *Ballet Review* vol. 1 no. 6 1967
CAROLYN BROWN: 'On Chance' in *Ballet Review* vol. 2 no. 2 1968
BENJAMIN HARKARVY—unpublished interview with the author

Index